# How Chuck Taylor Got What He Wanted

**SECOND EDITION**

## (and how you can, too!)

by

William F. Staats
Professor of Banking and Finance
Louisiana State University

and

E. D. Sledge
President
Consumer Credit Counseling Services
Baton Rouge, Louisiana

# How Chuck Taylor Got What He Wanted

SECOND EDITION

(and how you can, too!)

Library of Congress Catalog Card Number:
95-71163

Published by Credit Counseling Services of Louisiana, Inc.
dba Consumer Credit Counseling Services
615 Chevelle Court
Baton Rouge, Louisiana
504-927-4274

Produced in cooperation with the
Council for Professional Education, Inc.

Printed and Bound in the United States of America

ISBN: 0-9627885-1-1                                    Price: $14.95

# How
# Chuck Taylor
# Got What
# He Wanted

**SECOND EDITION**

## (and how you can, too!)

The Second Edition of *How Chuck Taylor Got What He Wanted* has been donated to all high schools throughout the state of Louisiana for use as a supplemental text to regular classroom materials.

This book is dedicated to all of the responsible young adults who enter the American workforce and marketplace each year.

America's future is in their hands.

# ACKNOWLEDGMENTS

The authors would like to express their sincere gratitude to the following persons, organizations, and companies who have been of tremendous help and support in preparing this book.

### The CCCS, Baton Rouge, Board of Directors

The past and present board members of this organization have built a solid foundation for credit education becoming an integral part of the CCCS mission. Without their vision and leadership, CCCS could not play an important role in providing financial responsibility education to our next generation of consumers.

### Louisiana's School Systems and Their Officials, Principals, and Free Enterprise Teachers

Recognizing the importance of credit education, our state's educators have supported our initiatives with enthusiasm. We, the authors, can contribute educational tools, but it is ultimately the teachers and others in the system who deliver that information to the students.

### Charles A. Worsham, President & CEO of the Louisiana Bankers Association

Without Mr. Worsham's support and initiatives, we could not have achieved our goal to get this text donated to high schools throughout Louisiana. Our special thanks to Mr. Worham, the LBA, and its supportive members for helping to make this project successful.

*Gerald Garrison, Garrison & Associates Advertising and Public Relations, Inc.*

Mr. Garrison, without compensation, contributed countless hours of his time and professional assistance in promoting the sponsorship of this edition and the first. In addition, he greatly assisted CCCS in the tremendous challenge of preparing this book for print.

*Bayou GMC Truck Team Dealers*

For their generous sponsorship of the front cover.

*Sue Hughes of CCCS and Linda Rathburn of the Council for Professional Education*

Our special thanks to Sue and Linda for their tireless work with the countless details involved with such a project.

*The Financial Services Industry — the Creditors Who Support CCCS and Its Mission*

Not enough can be said here; no expression of thanks is adequate. These companies are the financial backbone of our free enterprise system. Recognizing consumers as people as well as customers, they provide the financial support and cooperation that makes every CCCS across the country a viable human service organization.

*Angèle D. Davis, Vice President of Education, Marketing, and Development, CCCS, Baton Rouge*

The authors owe a special debt of gratitude to Angèle. Right in the middle of many other responsibilities, Angèle coordinated all of the pre-press work for the text, including the design of the cover, facilitated communications with our many sponsors, and made sure that the countless other details were taken care of. Without her tireless efforts, this project would not have been a success.

William F. Staats
E. D. Sledge
Baton Rouge, Louisiana

# Table of Contents

# Introduction to the Second Edition

When Live comes up with a hit CD, people buy it. They buy it because they like it. Often, people buy all of the copies the recording company has made. In that case, the company makes some more. Like a second edition.

So it is with books. So it was with the first edition of this book. The demand for the first book was greater than anticipated. A second printing of the first book was ordered and donated to more schools. Now, a second edition has been written. You are holding a copy of the second edition.

The first edition proved the concept of this book. More than 11,000 copies of this book were put into the hands of high school students and their families. Companies such as McDonald's Restaurants, Exxon Federal Credit Union, Our Lady of the Lake Regional Medical Center, Baton Rouge Coca Cola Bottling Company, Gerry Lane Chevrolet, The Dow Chemical Company, Guaranty Bank (now Regions Bank), Louisiana Public Facilities Authority, Rapides Bank, and Calcasieu Marine National Bank believe in this book. They donated those 11,000 copies to high schools.

When we showed the first edition to potential sponsors in 1991, we were absolutely amazed by the remarks we encountered. Many said, "If I had just had a book like this when I was young, I could have avoided so many mistakes!" Such great interest in, and enthusiastic response to, that first edition made us really look forward to writing the second edition. We are thrilled to be able to help many more thousands of youth understand a bit of the financial world they are about to face.

# Introduction — Why Read This Book?

"Have you seen the new car Chuck Taylor just bought? That's a sharp car. It's just about as sharp as the one his sister got about a year ago. Those Taylor kids aren't much older than we are. How can they afford those wheels? What do they know that we don't?"

Well, Chuck and his sister must know something because dealers don't just give away cars! What Chuck and his sister know is in this book. That's why this could be one of the most important books you will ever read. This book tells you some financial facts of life and gives them to you straight. It tells you about the real world out there, in terms of your opportunities and your responsibilities.

Now, lots of things are tough out in the real world, and some of them aren't even fair. We may not like that, but that's the way it is. We all have to live in the real world. So, like Chuck and his sister, we are better off knowing exactly how things really are and how things really work in this real world.

The authors want you to have a chance to learn these things for a couple of reasons. First, believe it or not, our economic system is full of a lot of good business people. They are sincerely interested in you and your economic future. Second, they know that if you have the chance to learn some economic facts of life and can apply them, you will have a better life—a higher standard of living. Also, the whole economic system will be better off. We're all on this big boat together. The more people who can have a good ride, the better everyone else is. The more people who fail financially, the more the rest of us have to throw life rafts to them. That costs the rest of us money.

Many, if not most, of the readers are going to learn something from this book and be better off. A few will learn a lot. They will use that knowledge all though their lives. Some readers will just browse through this book. When they find out it may not be as entertaining as the latest rock video, they may just "tune out." Those who tune out now will have some very painful lessons later in life!

In this book, we focus on the way things are. Many of us may not like the way some things are in this world, but that's beside the point. Maybe, someday, you will be motivated to change things for the better. In the meantime, we have to exist. That doesn't mean that we have to conform to all things all the time. However, we all have to play by some important rules that have been in place for a long time. There are certain economic realities which are just as much facts of life as are the facts about sex. We are not telling you how the world ought to be, but how it is.

In 1965 Consumer Credit Counseling Services was organized by the business community as a non-profit service to provide advice and counseling to people who found themselves over their heads in debt. Back then, counselors at CCCS rarely saw a young person in financial trouble, because young people could not easily borrow money. That's all changed. Now, people are offered the opportunity to establish credit at a much younger age, often in their late teens. Generally, this is a good thing, as many young adults are ready to handle the responsibilities of using credit. But, many others are not. CCCS counselors often see 18 and 19 year olds who owe 10 or more creditors as much as $20,000 or $25,000. Usually all they have to show for that debt is a car with a mortgage for more than the car is worth! They face several years of sacrifice to pay for their mistakes.

These young people have two things in common: (1) none of them sets out to mess things up on purpose; and (2) all of them ask, "How did this happen to me?" CCCS is able to help most of these young adults. Others may end up in bankruptcy court, branded as a financial failure very early in their lives. Often, that failure could have been avoided had they learned what you have a chance to learn now from this book. Many young people make serious mistakes handling financial decisions and credit responsibility. They just never learned how to make the right decisions regarding money and credit. At a time in their lives when needs (and wants) are the greatest, their income is the smallest. If they do not learn how to use credit wisely, they are likely to get into serious financial trouble that will haunt them for years. These people are not bums, and they aren't stupid either. They just don't know all they need to know. They don't know the things in this book.

By the way, we don't believe that learning has to be boring. We think that a serious subject can still be fun to learn. We've tried to make this book as light and lively as possible. Of course, just like the real world, this book has some tough parts in it.

We show you how Chuck Taylor got much of what he wanted — not everything, but at least some things. We explain the basic economic and financial engine that runs our system. We explain economic wants and desires. We tell you why everyone cannot have everything that he or she desires. Also, we explain who gets to have the things such as cars, nice clothes, a fine house or an apartment, and other things that are produced in our economic system.

You have a chance to learn what you have to know and what you have to do in order to play the game of life successfully—at least that part of life that deals with money. You will get a chance to learn what credit can and cannot do for you, and how to get your credit started. You'll learn why savings are so important—important enough to give up something now for something better later.

As you go through life, this knowledge will help you get more of what you need and want. As a result of this knowledge, you will have the opportunity for a better standard of living. Whoever said that money is not everything in life was right. But money sure helps, and so do the finer things in life that you can have by managing the money you will earn.

# Part I

# The Basics of Money and the Marketplace

# Building a Foundation of Knowledge of the System

*Building Knowledge Is the Foundation*
*for Economic Success*

# Chapter One

# What People Want and
# What They Need

Remember when you believed in Santa Claus? You would make a list of things you wanted Santa to bring at Christmas. Chuck Taylor used to have such a list. He said that it was always a long list! There was practically no end to the things Chuck wanted. Most of us were like Chuck. Sometimes we got some of what was on our list, but seldom did we get everything.

Years have passed since most of us found out that the chubby guy in the red suit really didn't exist. Yet we still have a long list of things we want. Don't make a "Christmas" list, but take a minute and write down on a piece of paper eight or ten things that you would like to have right now.

Chances are that each person making such a list will have different items on it. More than likely, no two lists will be the same. There may be some things that are on nearly every list. Probably everyone will have at least one thing that doesn't appear on anyone else's list. All of us share some common wants or needs. All of us, however, are different and have unique wants and needs.

On many lists will be things such as happiness, health, love, and peace. Probably most of the things on your list are "goods." These are tangible things, such as a car, clothes, a digital sound system, or maybe your own apartment. For some reason, most of us think about goods or possessions when we think of a list of wants or needs. But there is more.

On some lists will be other things, such as medical care, hair styling, good government—these are called "services." They, along with goods, are what make up our economic standard of living. Services are sometimes more important than goods. We often don't think about services when we think about our wants and needs—unless our car is in the shop!

*People's Wants Are Unlimited*

## Necessities of Life

There are some things (whether they appear on our list or not) that we simply must have. These are "needs"—called the necessities of life. Examples would be food, shelter, clothes, and medical care. Some might argue that a good car should rank right up there near the top! A car is a necessity for some, such as those who use one in their work. Others would have no way to get to work other than by a private car. Most teens would argue that they have to have one, but a lot of them would have a tough time proving it.

## Luxuries of Life

At the other end of the scale are "wants" such as luxury goods and services. Examples of these wants might be a stay at a fancy resort, a diamond ring, and a membership in a health club or a spa. Luxury goods and services are not necessary for survival, and they tend to be expensive. We can all live quite well without them, but they sure are great to have. They can improve the quality of a person's life, *provided that the person can afford to buy them.*

## "In-Between" Goods and Services

Not everything can easily be lumped into one category or the other. Many items fall in between needs and wants. However, some could argue that anything that is not a necessity must therefore be a luxury. How each of us views luxuries depends on our own financial condition and our own values. A wealthy student might think that he or she can't get along without steaks or designer jeans. Another student might think that those things were ridiculous luxuries. Many young people in poor third-world nations would think that school itself was a luxury to dream about.

In the United States we tend to take our standard of living for granted. The very poorest of us would be seen as very rich by millions of people in the world. Because the more we have the more we want, we often fail to appreciate what we do have. Thanks to our U.S. economic system, we have more opportunities to get more goods and services than most people in the world have. But while most of us *can* have more, it's unlikely that most of us will ever get all we want.

Read on to learn the rules of the game. Chuck Taylor learned these things. As a result, he is making great progress in meeting more of his needs and fulfilling more of his wants.

## THINGS TO REMEMBER

*Needs* are goods and services which everyone must have to live or survive. They are basic necessities.

*Wants* are those goods and services which people desire to have, but are not necessarily needed for survival. They are luxuries.

There are things which cannot always be accurately classified as either a necessity or a luxury. These are the "in-between" goods and services.

People in the United States enjoy more goods and services than do most of the people in the world.

# Chapter Two

# Why Everyone Can't
# Have Everything

Even though Chuck is driving around in his new car, the truth is that he really wanted a Porsche. That has always been Chuck's dream, and maybe it will be for a long time. Right now Chuck can't handle the sixty-five "grand" that a Porsche costs! So his desire remains just that — a desire, maybe even a goal. More on goals later.

There are two reasons that most of us have unfulfilled wants on our list. First, we don't have enough money to buy everything we want. Second, there are not enough goods and services in the whole world to satisfy the desires of everyone. Not everyone can have everything he or she wants. Most of us have the potential in life to have a lot more than we have now. Chances are, however, that none of us will have everything we want. In the sections following, we explain why this is true.

## Production

In the Old Testament of the Bible there is a story that goes something like this. God sent the whole Israelite community in a mass escape from Egypt across the Red Sea and into the desert. Moses was the leader. There wasn't much going on in the desert at the time. No one was trucking in water, and no Red Cross was airlifting supplies. The people complained to Moses, fearing that they were going to starve to death. Then God caused food, called manna, to rain down from the sky. The people had only to pick it up and eat it.

Except for that one instance, throughout human history people have had to produce what they wanted and needed.

Air seems to be freely available; but with pollution today, even clean, healthy air is costing us a price. The car Chuck is enjoying had to be produced. The clothes we are all wearing right now had to be made. The schools had to be built, and the food we eat had to be grown. Somebody made the movies we watch.

Some people, including many politicians, often behave as if just wishing for more goods and services would automatically create them. It just doesn't work that way. For us to have and enjoy goods and services, they must first be produced. If no one is willing to work to produce these things, then they will not be available. That is a basic economic fact of life. Everything has to be produced, and production depends on *factors of production.*

## Factors of Production

To produce any good or service, we need five types of things: *labor, capital, resources, technology,* and *land.* Even with all of these, we need one more thing—entrepreneurship, which we describe later. Everything that is produced consists of some combination of these factors. In fact, the only thing that makes one good or service different from another is that different types of each of the factors are combined in the production process. This book, your clothes, and your car (if you have one), however different, were each produced by a combination of the five factors of production. In the United States, we are fortunate because we have an abundance of the *factors of production.*

### Labor

Labor is one of the most familiar factors of production because we know that most people work. Without labor, everything grinds to a halt. Even highly automated machines cannot function without human labor. First the machines are invented, and then they are manufactured. Then they must be maintained, and finally replaced when they wear out.

There is one overwhelming reason for people to work: work brings reward. That reward is called a paycheck — money! That reward makes it possible for workers to buy goods and services. And for most of us, a sense of accomplishment is another type of reward we get from working.

Production of things such as a house or a work of art requires a lot of labor. Other things, such as notebook paper, can be produced with very little labor. The key point is that some labor is a necessary input for every good or service.

On the job, Chuck Taylor works. Chuck's labor is required to produce something. If Chuck doesn't show up for work, production slows. Chuck and all other workers perform an important function, whatever the job is.

**Workers Are Needed to Produce Goods and Services**

### Capital Goods

Labor alone is not enough to produce goods and services. Workers need tools, equipment, and factories to work in. We call these things capital goods. Even in the most primitive economies, workers need capital in order to produce something. For example, the early American Indian hunters needed bows and arrows to hunt meat to eat. Farmers need tractors, truckers need trucks, plumbers need wrenches, steel workers need blast furnaces. The list goes on and on.

### Resources

Without raw materials to work with, no goods can be produced. The Indian with the best bow and the most arrows needed resources in the form of deer and the other wild animals. Today, we could not produce clothes, cars, or anything else without raw materials.

Resources are natural things that are required in the production of every good or service. Among the common resources are wood, iron ore, oil, and coal. Our world is blessed with abundant, but often abused, resources.

**Resources Are Needed to Make Goods**

## Technology

All the labor, capital, and resources in the world would not result in production of any goods or services without technology. "Know-how" is another term for technology. Corning Ware, those bowls in our kitchens, was not produced until we learned how from the U.S. program of space exploration. During the days of the horse and buggy, the resources existed to produce automobiles. But cars could not be made until someone developed the technology for the internal combustion engine. Before the price of autos could be reduced enough for many families to afford them, Henry Ford had to develop the technology of the production line.

It is easy to overlook technology or take it for granted. But we must realize that nothing can be produced without "know-how." Also, to increase the efficiency of production, we must continually improve technology. If you want to increase the value of your labor (so you will receive greater rewards), you must learn new things and improve your skills. That way, you can produce more and better things and your labor will be worth more. You will get to enjoy more goods and services.

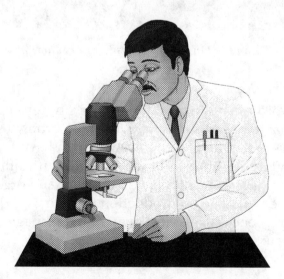

**Technical Skills Are Needed to Produce Goods and Services**

### Land

Of course, we need a place where we can bring together the first four factors of production. That place is land. However, it could be on the sea as in the case of a floating fish factory. Maybe one day it will be in the form of an orbiting space station! But even if the sea and space are used in production, we still need some old fashioned land. We need a place for the ships to dock as well as a place to launch and land the spaceships. Land, then, is a factor of production.

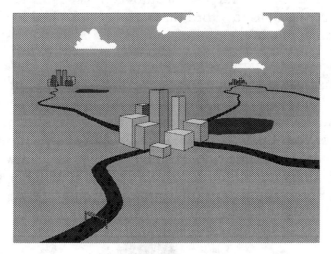

*Land Is One of the Factors of Production*

### Entrepreneurship

This word is hard to pronounce. Try "on-trey-pray-newer-ship." What it means is the creative act of putting together the five factors of production. You see, we can have lots of land, labor, capital, resources, and technology. But until someone takes the initiative to put them all together and organizes the activity, we will have no production. People who do that are called entrepreneurs. Business owners and managers often are entrepreneurs.

## Wants and Scarcity

We need very little to exist. Food, water, air, shelter, and of course, love and attention from other people are necessary. But everyone wants more than just a basic existence. In fact, if people were to list everything they really wanted, some would never stop writing.

Many or most of our wants will never be satisfied because the factors of production are limited. There is only so much labor available, so much capital, so many resources, and so much technology. Therefore, there is a limit as to how much can be produced. We have unlimited wants, but limited resources to produce those things. However, as people become more educated, labor becomes more productive. Resources can be used more efficiently as technology is advanced. Better education results in a better standard of living for working people.

## How Much Gets Produced?

The answer to the above question should be simple. We produce all we can. But it doesn't work that way. People may choose to produce less than the greatest amount possible. People trade off labor for vacation. Sometimes we leave some lands unspoiled rather than use the resources from them. These are only two examples that show that we often produce less than the greatest possible amount of goods and services.

We may choose to limit production in many ways, but we cannot produce more than the *factors of production* will allow. It has been estimated that the factors of production increase by roughly five percent a year. New natural resources are discovered, land is developed and made usable, labor becomes more productive, and technology is improved. This means the maximum amount of goods and services that can be produced can expand by only that same five percent each year. Despite what some politicians seem to preach, not everyone can have everything he or she wants!

Because things are scarce, they have value. The scarcer something is, the more value it has. If gold could be found anywhere, jewelry would be cheaper. Perhaps, then, we would not want it as much. The concept of scarcity and value is a simple one, but very important. Understanding this concept helps us to understand many other economic facts of life.

## What Gets Produced?

Because of the limits on total production in the economy, we have to decide what specific goods and services get produced. In socialistic or communistic countries, government officials decide what will be produced. A relatively small group of people make the decisions. In a market economy, such as ours, *we* decide what gets produced. Did you know that? We buy what we decide we need and want the most. Therefore, that's what companies will make.

Each of us, by our actions in the marketplace, helps decide what goods and services are produced. When we quit buying buggy whips for horse carriages, factors of production were no longer channeled to making that product. When we started wanting and buying the new cellular telephones, more labor, capital, resources, and technology were directed toward increased production of that product. People obviously want a cure for AIDS. Factors of production are being channeled toward finding that cure.

As you and Chuck and I spend money, we are *voting in the market* for what we want produced. The economy responds to that spending by using the factors of production to produce the things we want.

But remember, there are limits of production. If our demand for a product increases faster than the factors of production, prices will go up. However, if one or more of the factors of production are increased, prices will go down. For example, good quality TVs and VCRs are cheaper today than they were 10 years ago largely because of the advances in technology.

Chuck Taylor's new car is a combination of the factors of production. Labor, capital, resources, and technology were combined and resulted in a car. The steel that went into Chuck's car could not also be used to make another product. The same is true for the other factors of production.

In spending money to buy that car, Chuck was telling business people that he wanted those factors of production to go into the automobile. That is how each of us helps to decide what gets produced. That is also why we Americans have the highest standard of living in the world.

*Skills Mean Jobs — You Decide What We Produce*

## THINGS TO REMEMBER

The production of goods and services is dependant upon five factors of production: *land, labor, capital, resources,* and *technology.*

*Entrepreneurship* is the process of combining factors of production so that goods and services can be produced.

The supply of the factors of production can be increased within limits. If production is increased through better productivity and wiser use of resources, we are all better off.

There are not enough resources available for all of us to get everything we desire.

What gets produced in the marketplace in the U.S. is decided mainly as a result of what the people want. This is evidenced by what the people are most willing to spend their money on.

# Chapter Three

# Who Gets What Is Produced?

A lot of people would like to have Chuck Taylor's new car. In fact, some people may think that it's just not fair that they don't have one like it. When some people see others who have more goods and services than they have, they cry foul.

Sure! It would be great if everyone had a new car and everything else he or she wanted. But we pointed out in the last chapter that the economy simply cannot produce enough goods and services to satisfy everybody's wants. So, who gets what is produced? That's one of the hottest questions in our society. We find the answers in this part of the book.

## How the System Works

In the United States, most goods and services go to the people who have earned the money to purchase them. People like Chuck who work provide labor. As a reward for contributing to production, they get paychecks. Those paychecks and the money that they represent can be used to buy goods and services. And if we're smart, we'll stash a little of our income for a rainy day.

Some of our money is taxed away from workers and put into government welfare programs. This helps provide at least a minimum level of living for those who are unable to participate in the economic process. Some people cannot work because of some type of mental or physical impairment. Surely we have to take care of the people who would work if they were able. However, the productive portion of our society has limitations on how much of what it produces can be directed to a non-productive segment.

Without labor, as we saw earlier, there can be no production. Without production, there can be no goods and services. A system of rewards promises each of us that if we provide the labor needed to produce things, we can get more of what we want. If we work, we can get at least some of what is produced. Generally speaking, the more and better we work, the more we get.

*Chuck's Part-Time Job Helped Buy His Car*

Chuck's part-time job provided him with disposable income. Disposable income is income in excess of that required for necessities. At first, Chuck saved that disposable income toward a down payment. When he had enough savings to meet that goal, he bought the car. Then he began directing his disposable income to the monthly payments. In the meantime, some of his friends were just hanging around. Now, they envy his car and wish they had one too.

Chuck didn't make a lot of money when he first started on his job a few years ago. In fact, sometimes he wondered if it was worth it. But he kept working. In the process, he learned more about his job and how to be of more value to his employer. As his value increased, so did his pay. He's making even more now. And when he finishes his education, he's got a chance at earning some "big bucks."

It's a fact of life that not everybody is paid the same for the same hours of work. The value of labor depends on many things. There is a demand for people who have skills, knowledge, and experience. They will earn more than someone who is unskilled, undereducated, and inexperienced. Generally speaking, the more that someone can contribute to the economy, the more he or she will get out of it. That's the reward system.

Let's face it. Some people are a bit lazy. Many of them would like to take two six-month vacations each year! But if they don't work, they don't contribute anything to the production of goods and services. Hence, they don't deserve to have any of the goods and services that are produced by those who do work. Don't think for a minute that Chuck worked hard to see someone else get his new car. Would you? In this country, each person has the choice *not* to work. But those who choose not to work should have no claim on the goods and services that the rest of us work to produce.

## The Market

There is a market for just about everything. Every good and service can be bought and sold. The "market" does not mean just a place where buying and selling take place. The term market also describes how people behave in an economic way. We need to understand this market, because we are all a part of it. We are all actively buying and selling things. We sell our labor when we work. In our country, the market is the main way we answer the question, "Who gets what is produced?" By the way, the market is also the way we decide *what* gets produced and *how* those things are produced. Let's check that out.

When Chuck bought his new car, he sent a message to the market. That message said, "Make more cars. Allocate more factors of production to automobiles." Here is how that works. When demand for a particular good or service increases, the price of that item goes up in relation to the prices of other goods and services. In turn, that higher price attracts more of the factors of production. For example, if the *demand* for cars increases, the company making the cars needs more workers. That will tend to increase wages to attract additional workers. The same thing happens to the other factors of production: resources, capital, technology, and land.

When people stopped buying as many LPs and started buying more compact discs, factors of production shifted to meet the new demand. That increased the supply of compact discs. This was the result of our votes in the marketplace.

## Supply and Demand

The price, or value, of each factor of production, as well as the value of every good or service, is determined by two things: supply and demand. Here is a general rule that always works no matter what the good or service. The greater the supply relative to demand, the lower the price will be. The opposite is also true. If demand for some good or service increases and supply does not, the price will rise.

## Price

In the late 1980s, fast food stores like Burger King and McDonald's in parts of the northeastern U.S. were advertising for workers. The pay was around eight dollars an hour! That's a fairly high wage for jobs which don't require much skill and are available to high school students. Why was that pay so high? Well, there were more of those jobs available than there was labor willing to do that work. In other words, demand exceeded supply, so the price went up. We call the price of labor "wages."

In the early 1970s, the price of a gallon of gasoline was around 30 cents. Look at the price now. It is now around a dollar and a quarter a gallon. Here's what happened.

In 1974, the Arab nations which produce a very large part of the world's crude oil stopped selling that oil for a while. They wanted to drive the price up. It worked. By sharply reducing the supply of oil, from which gasoline is made, the price of gas increased. Later in the seventies, trouble in Iran caused a further decrease in the supply. The result was still higher prices at the pump.

During the late eighties, there no longer seemed to be a threat to the supply of oil. The price of oil dropped somewhat.

In 1990, the invasion of Kuwait by Iraq threatened the supply of crude oil. The immediate result was that the price of gasoline soared again. As soon as the U.S. and its allies forced Iraqi troops back where they belonged, the supply of oil was again secured and the market settled down.

On the demand side, we were producing and driving more cars. The population was growing; so, people bought more gasoline. Growing demand, then, also helped to push up the price of a gallon of gasoline.

Simply stated, the relationship of the supply of something together with the demand for that good or service determines the price.

*Oil Shortages Mean Higher Prices at the Gas Pump*

## Quantity

Supply and demand determine the amount of any good or service that is produced in our economy. At every price, say for gasoline, there is some amount that we will buy. As the price goes up, we buy less. As the price goes down, we buy more. That is called the "Law of Demand." That's not a law passed by Congress. It's a true statement about the market and how we behave with respect to price. No Congress or legislator can repeal the "Law of Demand." As the price of a good or service goes up, people who supply that good or service will put more on the market. At a lower price, they will put less on the market. Consumers generally will buy more of anything at a lower price, and less at a higher price.

That's how the market system works. Our economic activity is based on the market system. It works better than any other type of economic system in the world. People throughout history have tried other ways of deciding what should be produced, what should determine price, and who should get what is produced. No other system has worked as well as ours. In fact, communist nations such as the Soviet Union and China are moving toward the market system. They have accepted the fact that their old systems simply don't work as well as ours. Our system isn't perfect, but it is the best yet! It puts more goods and services into the hands of more people than any other system we know.

## Who Gets What Is Produced?

People who have money, or the opportunity to use credit, get what is produced. It's just that simple! The more money and income a person has, the more he or she can buy.

Remember, Chuck got what he wanted because he had the income and, thus, the opportunity to use credit. Others with no money or credit may have wanted that car just as much as Chuck. It is possible they may have needed it more. But Chuck was productive, and he got it.

Generally, people who work to help produce goods and services are the ones who can afford to buy. It's a fact that some people get paid more than others for their work. Let's see why that is.

There is a demand for and a supply of labor, as we stated in the previous pages. If you are able to provide the kind of labor that (1) is more in demand and (2) has fewer workers competing for that kind of work, your earnings will be higher. That's because of the supply and demand that we explained earlier. Check out Shaquille O'Neal and the amount of money he earns.

Because a limited number of people have a good education, good skills, and useful knowledge, the supply of such workers is relatively scarce. The demand, however, for these people is great. The result is a higher wage rate. Those people are able to contribute more to the production of goods and services. Therefore, they are rewarded by the market system with higher pay. Those are the folks with more money and credit. They get to buy more of what is produced.

**Hard Work Is Rewarded in the Marketplace**

## THINGS TO REMEMBER

In the U.S. economy, people decide what gets produced. They "vote" in the marketplace by buying goods and services.

The supply of and demand for goods and services (including labor) determines the market price.

People who have the most valuable knowledge and skills in the work force receive a greater proportion of the goods and services produced.

As demand for a good or service increases, the price of that good or service will increase unless supply can be increased.

If supply increases without an increase in demand, the price will drop.

# Chapter Four

# Who Are the Players That Win?

In this country's economic system, we are free to participate in the production of goods and services. In fact, if we really want any of those things on our want list, we have to play the game. Yes, life is serious, but it can be compared to a game. Those who prepare well and play to win usually are the winners. Some people cannot play because they are physically or mentally impaired. Their handicap is beyond their control. That's why those of us more fortunate support them through government welfare programs and through private charitable organizations.

Chuck had the game figured out. He had help. He had a chance to learn from some mistakes his older sister made. She had dropped out of high school with only a year to go. "Just got bummed out on school," she said. She had a tough time. No one would hire her for a good job with a chance for real advancement. She scratched out a few bucks here and there. She did it the hard way and without much reward. It was a real drag. She had little income and couldn't buy new clothes or many of the other things she needed, let alone wanted. Without the good pay that a decent job provides, she just didn't get to play.

Chuck saw his sister's problems, and he is sticking it out in school. In fact, he has worked part-time all through high school and college. By the way, his sister got her act together and went back to finish school. It was a lot harder, but by then she was just a little bit wiser. Now she has a job with a real future and is making good money.

*Think About a Winning Future*

## What Is Money?

We can make a good case that love makes the world go around. There is love for our family, for ourselves and friends, for our country, for the Supreme Being. Maybe love is the basic thing in life, but money is a close second. Let's face it—money is important.

All of us are around money most of the time. It is hoped that all of us have a little right now. But most people really don't understand exactly what money is and all that money does.

A lot of us think of money as nickels, dimes, quarters, and the "folding stuff." But coin and currency, as those things are called, make up only a little of our supply of money. Things other than coin and currency also serve as money.

If we wanted to define money, we must say that money is anything which is generally accepted as performing the *func-*

*tions of money.* That may sound a little fuzzy, but that is money. Money is anything people will accept as performing those things we expect money to do for us.

Weird things have been accepted as money in some societies. For example, in one of the South Pacific island societies, people used belts made of feathers from red birds which lived on the islands. Other strange types of money used in the past include rocks, beads, fur pelts from animals — and yes, even something called gold.

Some of these things that perform the functions of money today include checking accounts, travelers checks, savings accounts, and other things. All of these, along with coin and currency, are generally accepted as performing the functions of money.

## The Functions of Money

Money performs important functions for us and for the whole economy. We need to understand these functions so that we can use money properly.

### Medium of Exchange

The most obvious function of money is as a *medium of exchange*. That means that we can use money to buy goods such as a Pearl Jam or EarlyDawn disc, a pair of shoes, or a hamburger. Also, we use money to buy services, such as a haircut or car repairs. We exchange money for a service or a product. That's its function as a medium of exchange.

### Store of Value

Money does more than allow us to buy things. Most of us have saved money. In fact, if you have money in your purse or pocket right now, you have saved money. Perhaps you are saving money until you get enough together to buy a new set of stereo speakers. So, money serves as a *store of value*. In other words, we don't have to run out and exchange money for goods or services the moment we get it. Instead, we can hold it as a power to buy something in the future. This is simply called *saving*. When we are ready at sometime in the future, we can exchange the cash or part of our checking account or savings account balance for the goods or services for which we have been saving. In this way money serves as a store of value.

In effect, money represents a claim check. We can use it at any time. In the meantime, the money is acting as a storehouse of purchasing power. The function as a store of money is a pretty handy thing.

### Unit of Measurement

Money also serves as a *measure of value*. That's a fancy term for a measuring stick. We can use the measure of value to gauge incomes, prices, wealth, and things like that. When we compare a Chevy to a Porsche, we know one costs four times as much as the other. Also, we may know someone who earns twice as much income as another. Money allows us to express those different values in a very precise way. So money serves as a measure of value.

### Where Does Money Come From?

Chuck used to think that there was a fixed amount of money in the country. When one person received it, someone else had to give it up. Well, that's only partially true.

Chuck has worked part-time after school and on Saturdays. He noticed that when he got paid, he had that money and his boss no longer had it. He also noticed that later on Saturday nights, he no longer had all of the money. Someone else had the money he spent. It seemed to Chuck that the same amount of money was simply changing hands as people bought and sold goods and services.

Only later did Chuck learn that the amount of money in the country is not fixed. Rather, it gets larger as the need arises and smaller when the need is over. The supply of money in the U.S. expands and contracts as needed. How that works is beyond the scope of this book. We can tell you that something called the *Federal Reserve System* controls the ability of commercial banks to make loans to business firms as well as to us. In the simplest of terms, as loans are made by banks, the nation's money supply increases. As those loans are repaid, the money supply shrinks. While there is more to it than that, this really happens. It is not all that complicated.

## Why All of Us Can't Have All the Money We Want

If money is created when banks make loans, why can't we just require banks to lend money to everybody who needs some? Then we could have all we need! Unfortunately, that won't work. Here is why.

First of all, money by itself doesn't do anything for us. We can't eat it, nor can we wear it. It really has no value other than what can be bought with it. Money by itself does not determine our standard of living. Instead, it is the amount of goods and services over which we have control that determines our standard of living. Money is only the means that each of us uses to acquire those things which, in turn, determine our standard of living.

The problem is that there is a limited quantity of desirable things in this country and in all of the world. No matter what the politicians say or do, they cannot increase the supply of goods and services being produced.

Goods and services are scarce. The reason is that everything we want is a combination of resources and there are limits to the resources available. We just cannot produce everything we want. There simply is not enough labor, steel, plastic, land, or technology.

The politicians often imply that they are going to give people more money. Well, let's look at what would happen to our standard of living if the government simply gave every person in the country a million dollars!

Let's pretend that some politician made the rounds last night while we were all asleep. Let's say he dropped a suitcase with a million dollars at everybody's door. This morning, each of us woke up, and there it was. Wow! What would be the first thing you would do?

*How Would You Like a Million Dollars?*

If you were in school, you would probably "skip." But that wouldn't have mattered, because the school would be empty. Remember, everybody else got a million bucks also! Even the teachers. So, they probably would skip, too!

Remember that want list? High up on my list would be a new car. So I go down to the dealer with my suitcase for the model I've been wanting. Boy, would I be excited! But what would I find when I got there? I would find a long line of people, each hugging a suitcase full of cash. What has happened in just a few hours is that all of a sudden, the demand for cars, boats, houses, and everything else has increased. But the supply did not. All of a sudden, I realize that while the Santa Claus politician was running all over delivering suitcases, there were no little elves busy in the factories making things overnight.

So here I am at the dealership. Maybe that's you right ahead of me in the long line. What do you think is about to happen? Some guy back in the line is going to see that the dealer will run out of cars. So he shouts to a salesman waiting on somebody else, "Hey, I'll give you $10,000 over sticker for that red one!" Another guy with his eye on the red one hollers, "I'll give you $20,000 over!" In about 10 seconds, everybody in line is bidding up the price of the cars. They have plenty of cash, but the cars are scarce.

Don't forget, the same thing is happening all over town and all over the country. At every car dealership, boat place, furniture store, and everywhere else people have suitcases full of money. Every kid who's been wanting to get his own apartment is out on the street looking. But only the early birds would get the worm, because there are only just so many goods and services available. And guess what's happening to prices?

Literally, within minutes that morning, the price of everything in the country would have gone out of sight. It would probably take more than a million bucks to buy that car! Everyone would be worse off because the price of everything would be sky-high. That afternoon, when you got hungry, a hamburger would probably cost $100, if you could find one. Don't forget, very few workers showed up for work. The production of goods and services ground to a screeching halt.

The only part of this story that's a fairy tale is everyone getting the million dollars. If that would have happened, the results we discussed would be true. Too much money chasing too few goods drives prices up. That is called inflation.

Having more money does not necessarily mean that we are better off. Our standard of living depends not on how much money we have, but on the amount of goods and services we can buy with the money we have.

It's true that if the amount of money *you* have increases faster than the amount *other* people have, you will be better off.

One of your real-world challenges is to learn how to earn more so you can be worth more. Another, and very important, challenge is to learn how to use what you do earn intelligently. If you can earn more and use your money wisely, you are going to have a higher standard of living.

From this book you will be able to learn about some of the things that you can do to play the game and to be a winner. You need to learn how to earn a good income, how to use credit wisely, and how to manage your finances well. Then you can play the game as well as Chuck, or maybe even better.

## THINGS TO REMEMBER

Money can be anything that will perform the functions of money.

The functions of money are a *medium of exchange, a store of value,* and a *measure of value.*

Too much money in the economy causes inflation — that is, the price of goods and services increases.

It is not the number of dollars you have or earn that is important; rather, it is the amount of goods and services you can buy with the money you have that affects your standard of living.

Managing the money you do earn wisely is as important as earning money in the first place.

## Chapter Five

# Setting Goals, Making Choices, and Establishing Priorities

Everybody wants to be rich. Well, almost everybody. Most people are motivated to earn more, to achieve an ever higher standard of living. For some, however, money seems to hold little attraction. They are motivated by totally different things, and there's nothing wrong with that.

How do people accumulate wealth? A few seem to be born with a silver spoon in their mouth and to get everything handed to them on a platter. At least it seems like that to the rest of us. Usually, people who get ahead in life are able to do so because they have learned to set goals and work to attain them. This goes for athletic activities, financial well-being, and all other aspects of life.

We're not going to tell you to set your sights on being President of the United States. We're not even going to tell you that you should set the goal of becoming rich. If you want either (or both) of these goals, you had better read and learn a lot more than what is in this book.

We can tell you to set your sights on something worthwhile. Then go for it! That's what goal setting is all about. Your goal can be to be rich, to be happily married, to succeed in a career, or to tour the world. Most people have many goals; a few others, unfortunately, don't have any.

**Goals**

Some people never set goals. They just wander along through life, waiting for whatever comes along. There may be nothing wrong with this, but let's hope these people aren't waiting for good things to happen to them. A lot of people who don't set goals tend to be failure-prone and don't expect much out of life. It's not likely that you are this type of person, or you wouldn't have read this far in this book.

Another group of people set wildly unrealistic goals. They set themselves up for a failure or disappointment because they have set their sights too high. Of course, being ambitious is one of the keys to accomplishment. But patience and good judgment are just as important.

*Careful Planning Leads to Success in Whatever We Do*

Just setting your sights on something isn't going to make it happen. You must have a workable plan. And, you have to carry out that plan. A ladder without steps is useless. Even if it leaned against a strong tree, you couldn't climb it. This is the secret of smart goal-setting. Decide what you want, then build a ladder with steps that will get you there.

### Your Plan

A simple but effective trick in achieving your big goals is to identify and set intermediate sub-goals or steps. Those steps must be designed like the steps on a ladder leading straight to where or what you want to be. Let's say you want a new car like Chuck's. You can't simply say your goal is to have a new car and expect it to fall out of the sky. Wanting isn't enough! You must have a plan with several intermediate steps. The first step would be to get a job to earn money. The next step is to develop a savings habit so you could make a down payment. That requires self-discipline and budgeting, *and* doing without some other, perhaps less important, things so you don't spend all your earnings. The third step is to establish your credit if you haven't already. Establishing earning power and demonstrating your ability to save are the building blocks to establishing credit.

Needless to say, there has to be some common sense to your plan. It has to be realistic, or you set yourself up for disappointment. Let's say that right now you don't have much savings, nor do you have a large income. But you want a Ferrari. No amount of goal-setting will help you to pull that off anytime soon. Maybe your first goal should be to get a used car. After all, a clean used set of wheels would beat bumming rides. Intelligent and careful shopping can almost always result in finding good used transportation for very little money. Notice we said transportation. We didn't say the car of your dreams. But that first used car can help lead to a nicer one later on.

Just about everything in life worth having has to be worked for in one way or another. A happy marriage, or just a good relationship with another person, doesn't just happen accidentally. Success in a career rarely falls in anyone's lap. Owning a nice home one day won't happen just because you want it to. All of these things require goal-setting and a plan to make them happen. Then you must have the determination to make your plan work.

### Choices

No one gets everything he or she wants. We must choose some things over others. In fact, all through life we are faced with choices. We can choose to stay in bed or get up and see what challenges the day brings us. Making choices is related to goal-setting. We have to decide what we want the most. This is a process of setting priorities — deciding what is most important. Something always has to be sacrificed in order to get something else. No two people always have exactly the same priorities.

If you want a good education, say a college degree, then you usually have to put off a full-time job. But the reward for getting that degree is usually a lifetime of higher earnings and the potential of a better career path. Saving the down payment for a car means not spending some money on other things along the way. If you want a truly rich and rewarding relationship with someone, that also means sacrificing and not being selfish. This is true whether that person is one of your parents, a brother or sister, or a friend of the opposite sex.

There can be a hidden trap in making choices. Sometimes we make choices without really knowing what we are doing. We commit ourselves to things without realizing what we have done. Sometimes we accidentally or carelessly make the most important choices. A simple example is impulse buying. Maybe you have a little extra money, and you're in the mall one day. You went for a pair of shorts, but before you knew it, you spent more than a hundred bucks for a new pair of fancy athletic shoes. And, you bought the shorts. The point is that now you no longer have the choice of what to do with that hundred bucks. You already made it.

A far more serious example could be education. There are too many people who dropped out of high school. At the time, they probably had no plan for success, no goals for achievement. School seemed like a drag. So they dropped out of school. They made a serious choice in life without realizing the consequences. Later, when things got tough and they couldn't find a good job, they realized the mistake. This happened to

Chuck's sister. But unlike most dropouts, Chuck's sister had the intelligence, and the courage, to go back to school.

The bottom line is that successful and happy people do not get that way by accident. They set goals, make choices, and establish priorities in everything they do. Not just in how they spend their money or what kind of car they buy, but in *everything* they do. When they set goals, they strive to achieve them. When they make choices, they do so after carefully considering the options. And they think about the consequences of each choice. When they establish priorities, they are often making choices in their goals.

One thing more—nobody gets out of this life without making mistakes. Some are minor, but many are major ones. What sets some people apart from others is that they see and admit the mistakes they make and learn from them. Then they back up and, using the lessons they have learned, go in another direction. The next time they run into one of life's problems, they are wiser.

As you read further in this book, you are going to learn about how to make yourself of value in a job, what credit is all about, and how to establish and use your credit. We hope you see how the lessons in this chapter will affect you and your life in the future.

## THINGS TO REMEMBER

Usually, people who get ahead in life are able to do so because they have learned to set goals and work to attain them.

Have a workable plan to achieve the goals you do set. Do not set unrealistic goals.

No one gets everything he or she wants. We must choose some things over others.

Sometimes we make choices without realizing it. A failure to recognize choices when they present themselves can be a serious trap.

Everyone makes mistakes. Some people recognize and admit mistakes and can learn from them. Others do not and repeat them.

# Part II

# Earning Money and Using Credit

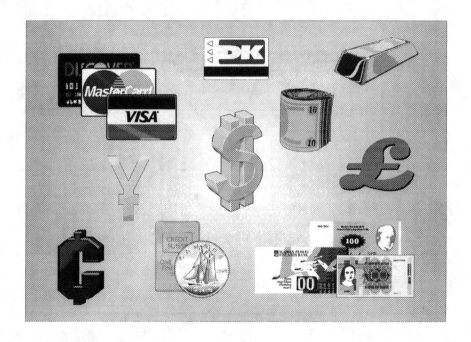

## Chapter Six

# How You Get Money

We all know how people get money. They either earn it, borrow it, steal it, or someone gives it to them. There are only a few who try to steal it, and all of them regret it when they have to pay their dues in jail. So let's leave out the stupid thief, and let's leave out the lucky person who gets money as a gift. That only leaves two ways to get money. In this chapter, we tell you some key things to help you earn more money and borrow wisely. In fact, we tell you just what Chuck did, because he's on the right track to a good life.

The only legitimate way to get money is to earn it by working for someone else, by owning your own business, or by receiving returns on investments such as savings. You can also borrow money, but it has to be paid back.

### Earning Money

Today, if you are a student in school, you may not be working. But your turn will be here before you know it, and you will be in the job market. If you are already working, you are beginning to experience some of what we are talking about. Even if you've been working for just a while, you've learned that it's a big world out there. And if you want to get ahead, there's a lot more you need to learn.

### What It Takes to Get a Job

Do you remember these two factors of production, labor and technology? To get a job, these are two factors that directly apply to each of us. We must be willing to work (to provide the labor), and we need some knowledge or know-how (technology). Generally speaking, the more you know, the better the jobs available to you.

*Skilled Labor Is in High Demand*

As we mentioned, Chuck's sister dropped out of school before getting her diploma. The result was that she had limited skills. The only jobs she could get didn't pay much. With only a little knowledge, she couldn't make much of a contribution to the economy; so her reward in terms of pay was very small. Finally, she did go back and finish school. Then she was able to get out of the low-pay trap.

Today, many people going to work have college degrees. Competition for good jobs can be tough, especially for someone who does not have much knowledge or training. To get a decent job, you need at least a high school diploma unless you like the idea of slinging hamburgers all of your life. A lot of people have made it big without a college degree. They worked hard. Along the road of success they learned how to be of value. That's what it's all about—learning to be of value. A college degree can help pave the road, but even having five degrees is a waste unless a person is willing to work hard.

When competing for that first real job, it helps a lot to have had part-time experience. This is true whether you have to go to work right out of high school or after finishing college. Working part-time during school teaches you a lot, and it tells the prospective employer that you know what work is all about.

Chuck's part-time job plus his education helped him land a very good job. It also taught Chuck the importance of:

- showing up for work and showing up on time;

- being neat and dressed for the job;

- working with and getting along with other people;

- being able to produce and be of value; and

- managing his time and money.

Getting to work on time is basic. An employer must be able to count on workers being there and being on time. A poor record of tardiness or absenteeism can cost an otherwise good employee a promotion, and worse, his or her job.

Wearing the proper clothes on the job is important. It is a reflection of maturity and responsibility. Every employee is a representative of his or her employer, and the worker's appearance is important.

More than one person has lost his or her job because he or she could not get along with others. Not being able to get along with others is also an indication of immaturity and irresponsibility. An employer cannot be expected to tolerate this type of problem in the work-place.

Productivity, along with all the other necessary traits, is the result of working hard and smart. It is why people are paid for their labor and their knowledge. Chuck learned quickly to be of value to his employer.

For Chuck, working and being productive meant managing his time well. This trait carried over to all other aspects of Chuck's life, including managing his money well. That's why he was able to save his down payment for the car. That's also why he is always able to make his payments on time.

There is something else important about getting a job and getting ahead. This is the simple habit of looking a person in the eye when talking to him or her. Eye contact is important whether you are applying for a job or just making a good impression on someone. Even if a person is well-dressed, intelligent, and skilled, he or she cannot make a good impression without eye contact. And don't forget to smile!

## What It Takes to Keep a Job

Getting a job is just the first step. You have to keep it. People can lose jobs for a lot of reasons. These are four main ones:

- they do something dishonest;

- they are not responsible or reliable;

- they are simply not worth what they are paid; or

- the company gets into financial trouble.

The first reason is easy to understand. An employer is not going to tolerate dishonesty, whether it's stealing or lying.

Being responsible and reliable — well, that's not so clear all the time. Some people are able to fool themselves. They convince themselves that they are responsible when their behavior says they are not. We often like to blame others when we mess up. If you fail an exam, it's easy to say, "The teacher didn't teach me that." Well, a teacher cannot teach you anything; all he or she can do is help you to learn. It's the same on the job. We can blame the boss or other workers for our mistakes. We can blame the traffic when we are late. But the bottom line is that we are responsible for what we do — or don't do.

In the very first part of this book, we said we were going to tell it like it is. We said that a lot of things are not fair — or at least they don't seem to be. This business of being paid what you are worth is a perfect example. There is probably no such thing as people being paid exactly what they are worth. We suspect that two conditions about pay exist in the marketplace. Some people are overpaid, and some are underpaid. Those who are overpaid are in trouble. Sooner or later, their jobs will be gone. Perhaps the safest position to be in is to be worth more than you are paid. That way you have no place to go but up!

*Learning Never Stops*

## How to Grow In a Job

Some people think the learning process stops when they get out of school. This is not true! Everyone is always learning, or at least they should be. The trick is to take advantage of the constant opportunities for learning and put what you learn to work. That way you are always improving, always growing. And your value in the job increases.

Chuck learned that quickly. He reads and keeps up with what is going on in the world. He found a couple of business magazines that focus on his type of work. He knows that if he wants to earn more, he must be worth more. He is always trying to increase his know-how. Chuck constantly increases his value to his job as he increases his knowledge in general. One day he may want to change jobs, and he knows he has to be ready.

## Earning Money — Working for Yourself

Working for the other person isn't the only way to earn money. While it may be the best way for many people, lots of others make it big on their own as entrepreneurs. It's not easy starting and running your own business. In fact, a lot of people who have big ideas about running their own business wind up broke. Generally, these are the dreamers looking for the easy way, and those who were not prepared. A lot of them wouldn't do well in a regular job either.

Most of us start out working for someone else — someone who is a successful business person. There is the opportunity to learn and earn — and to save money. Also, working in a job creates an environment for meeting people and building a good reputation. It takes all of these things for success.

To be successful in your own business, you have to have the technology — the know-how. To start most businesses, it takes a lot of money — working capital. There are two main reasons for most business failures. They are poor management and not enough capital to see the business through to the point of success. Chuck hopes to own his own business one day. He knows he is making money for his employer now. That's fine for the present. He hopes one day to be making that money for himself. But Chuck knows that starting a business is risky. He knows that a business owner faces tremendous challenges and risks. That's why the rewards can be great for the successful person. Chuck is going to be patient, learn all he can, and prepare himself. One day, just maybe, he will take the big plunge.

## Another Way of Earning Money—Return on Savings

Besides working for your money, you can have your money work for you! Here's how that works. First, you save some of your money instead of spending it all. Second, you put those savings to work for you. Usually this would be in the form of a savings account earning interest. You would not be the first young adult to invest and enjoy dividends and capital gains. We explain what these terms mean next.

*Chuck Saves Part of His Income*

### Interest

When you put some of your money in a savings account at a financial institution, such as a commercial bank, savings and loan association, or credit union, you are paid interest. You, in effect, are lending money to that institution. They will pay you to use your money. Typically, small passbook savings accounts earn at least 3 percent interest per year. On a savings account that had an even $100 in it the whole year, you would earn a little more than $3.

Why a little more? Because of something called compounding. That's where the interest owed you is calculated each day or each month. That interest is added to your account, and your interest for the next period is calculated on the new and higher amount in your account.

Interest may not sound like much on $100, but on larger sums it really adds up. If you have a larger amount in savings, often the interest rate can be higher.

This is a good place to describe a "Certificate of Deposit." That's where you have a large sum, usually $1,000 or more, that you agree to leave on deposit for a stated period of time. The institution will pay you a much higher rate of interest. This is because it is a larger amount, and you leave it there for a known period of time.

### Dividends and Capital Gains

Many people invest in the stock market. In this case, a person buys shares in the ownership of a company. That person actually becomes one of the owners of the company. While there can be a large potential gain if the company does well, there is also increased risk. If the company makes money, it may pay out part of its profits to shareholders in the form of "dividends." If the company really does well, the stock will increase in value because more people want to buy it. This increase in value represents "capital gains" to the investor. Of course, the stock can lose value. It can make you a nervous wreck as you watch the value move up and down!

Usually, people should only invest in stocks after they have a good chunk of regular savings in a safe place. This way they can afford to take more risk with a part of their assets.

### Borrowing Money

From time-to-time we may need to buy something before we have saved enough cash. Maybe we have some savings but don't want to touch them. There can be many situations, such as a medical emergency or major car repairs, which cause us to borrow. Also, we may wish to use something while we pay for it. We figure that the present use of the item, such as an auto (like Chuck's), is worth making payments and paying interest. Often, a smart investor will borrow money to invest. He had better be smart! Borrowing for legitimate purposes is fine, so long as borrowing is not abused.

How much a person can borrow is determined by several things. Often the most important of these are called "The Three Cs" — Character, Capacity, and Capital. (In lending, "capital" may include "collateral," or something of value that one mortgages as security for a loan.) Character may be the most important. This is a person's reputation. An example would be how promptly they paid their bills in the past. This is often determined by a "credit report." Later in this book we devote an entire chapter to explaining the role of credit bureaus. Capacity is a person's ability to repay credit, as determined by his or her "disposable income." Disposable income is income which is not needed for living expenses or already committed for other debt. The last of the three Cs, Capital, is often worth the least. Most reputable companies will not extend credit based just on collateral. Character and Capacity must also be present. Often one's Capital, used as collateral, is required in addition to the first two important qualities.

Collateral is something of value, such as a car, a home, or savings, that is pledged as security on a loan. When you finance a car or boat or anything else, that property, which now belongs to you, becomes collateral. This means that the creditor has a "lien" on the item. If you don't pay as agreed, the lender can take the collateral away from you.

But the collateral may not always pay off the whole remaining debt. If the car is "ragged" out and not worth what is owed on it, the creditor may sue you for what is called a "deficiency." In that case, you could lose the car and *still owe money!*

A lot of good folks get into serious trouble because they don't understand this. A person must realize the bank or credit union or finance company, or whoever extended the credit, isn't in the business for the collateral. They are in the money business. That's what they loaned out, and that's what they want back — plus interest.

The better the credit record (Character), the higher the income (Capacity), and the better the collateral (Capital), the more credit for which a person can qualify. Unless you have an excellent long-time credit record and have fantastic earnings, you better forget about the Porsche and go for the Chevy.

A down payment can be important when you are borrowing money to buy a big-ticket item, such as a car. The lender wants to know that you are using some of your own money. Now, you may see and hear a lot of ads claiming no money is needed for a down payment. On the bottom of the TV screen, however, a quick and small message flashes — "with approved credit." What that means is your credit better be very good!

Chuck borrowed part of the purchase price of his car. He didn't have a whole lot of credit because of his age. But he had saved a good down payment, and he had a stable earnings record. In another part of this book, we talk about some more important facts of using credit and borrowing money.

**Managing Money**

Once you get money by earning it, you have to use it wisely. "A fool and his money are soon parted." That's an old saying. It's still true today and will be as long as there are fools with money. In a later chapter, we tell you how to develop a savings program. We also talk about how to establish relationships with creditors and how to use money services. You also need to know how to protect yourself with insurance. Insurance is so important in life that we devote an entire chapter in this book to it.

One of the guys Chuck works with has a very high-paying job. But he doesn't have much to show for it. He doesn't pay any attention to his business. In spite of making good money, he is constantly going from one money problem to another. In fact, on occasion, he tries to borrow enough money from Chuck to get by till the next payday. And Chuck is only working part-time while he is in school!

There are two things that counselors at Consumer Credit Counseling Services can tell you as facts. There are a lot of people out there with a good standard of living who have never made a lot of money. There are also a lot of people always in trouble because they can't manage a high income.

*You Don't Need a Crystal Ball to Manage Your Money—A Well-Planned Budget Is Usually All That Is Needed*

Managing money is often called budgeting. Both terms simply mean planning in advance what you will do with a resource before you do it. You can't budget what you have already spent. You've already lost the choices. So if you are going to budget, or plan, you must do it in advance.

Many people make a simple but serious mistake in budgeting. They try to account for every penny, or plan things out down to the last cent. That's unnecessary, and it becomes discouraging when they find it is a lot of work. You must leave a little leeway, because no plan can be perfect.

A simple budget can be quickly and easily made. A recommendation is to make a budget for a consistent period, such as a month. Next, divide the month into paydays (unless you get one paycheck a month). Then develop a simple budget for each payday within the month. If you have *monthly* bills, you must assign them to a certain payday within the month. For each payday, start by setting aside the correct amount to pay things you are obligated to pay, such as a debt, and for essentials, such as food, shelter, and transportation expense. Whatever is left is *discretionary, or disposable, income*. Let's hope there is something left! You should set aside some part of discretionary income for savings.

**Start Your Savings Habit While You're Young**

If you develop a savings habit when you are young, it will stick with you for the rest of your life. You will reap the rewards of that habit later. It is very unusual for someone with a good savings habit to get into financial trouble. The amount, or percent, of your income that you set aside for savings can be flexible, but most experts recommend at least six to eight percent of your income. After determining your savings goal, you can make decisions about how you want to spend the remainder of your income.

A budget should be a living, flexible tool. Life seldom stays the same for long. Therefore, you must be ready to modify your budget as your circumstances change.

People often ask credit counselors how much of their income they should spend for what. But there is no simple answer. No two people are alike. Different people have different values, different priorities. Thank goodness—otherwise we would all wear uniforms and eat the same foods! In budgeting, you must decide what is most important for you. Just remember, you can't make each of your wants a top priority. Something has to give.

If clothes are the most important thing in your life, that's fine. Just be willing to drive a cheaper car. If a fancy apartment, or home, is sacred to you, that's all right too. But if you want it all, then you better set your career sights high and make yourself of great value. Otherwise you're in for a real crash.

## THINGS TO REMEMBER

Money is earned by working for someone else, owning your own business, or from receiving returns on investments.

Having a good work ethic is essential to keeping a job.

In order to borrow money, one must have *character*, *capacity*, and *capital*.

Starting your own business requires knowledge and capital.

The most common reasons for the failure of a new business are a lack of capital and poor management.

To be secure in a job, you should strive to be worth more than you are actually paid.

A high income does not guarantee a good lifestyle. Income must be managed wisely.

## Chapter Seven

# What Is Credit?

In this chapter, we tell you what credit is, how to get it, and — what's most important — how to use it wisely.

Right now, Chuck Taylor is a senior in college. He has worked part-time since he was in high school. We've already told you a lot about him and how he managed to buy that new car. Yes, he used credit. But he used it wisely.

Just about every time you turn on the TV or pick up a newspaper, some merchant is advertising how easy it is to use your credit. Advertising makes it sound good, doesn't it? Credit is good if it is used wisely. In fact, credit is just about the most powerful tool available to the average consumer. It can help us manage our income and have a good standard of living. But credit is just like any other powerful tool. It can hurt you if you don't use it safely.

Let's stop here and define the terms "credit" and "having good credit." *Credit* is created when someone gives you money or something else of value in exchange for your promise to pay at some time in the future. Probably every young person's experience with credit starts with borrowing from Mom or Dad against next week's allowance. Perhaps a friend may ask you to lend him five dollars in exchange for his IOU. Often these informal extensions of credit are simply oral agreements. Nothing is written down on paper. But when you go to the bank to borrow money, the banker will have you sign a legal loan agreement with specific terms. Credit is created in each of these instances.

The phrase *having good credit* means that the person who has good credit can borrow readily. This person has demonstrated that he or she has the capacity and character to be trusted to repay as promised. In the U.S. economy, credit is widely available to those who can give evidence of their ability and willingness to repay as agreed.

Chuck obviously established good credit. Without good credit, he could not have bought that new car unless he waited until he saved the entire purchase price. Now he is enjoying the rewards that can come from having and using credit intelligently. He is getting to drive the car while he is paying for it.

A *creditor* is the one who extends credit. It could be a parent, a department store, or a bank. Again, the credit is extended in return for a promise to repay, plus interest, on specific terms. The person who gives the promise to repay is a *debtor*. That term is a little on the negative side, so the term *borrower* usually is used. We use these terms a lot in the next several pages.

It's pretty easy for most people to get credit these days. Just look at some of the advertisements. These advertisers want you to use credit so that they can sell more of their products or services. Extending credit can help all kinds of businesses increase their sales and profits. After all, that's what business is all about — sales and profits. Many other kinds of companies, such as banks, savings and loans, consumer finance companies, and credit unions, are actually in the business of selling the use of money.

Because credit can be so easy to get, a few people will bite off more than they can chew. Usually, these are people who never learned to budget and are likely to buy something suddenly without giving much thought to the purchase. They can really get themselves into trouble. We said that credit is a powerful tool and must be used with respect. People who abuse credit quickly find themselves with a lot of debt and sometimes little to show for it. Later, when they really need credit badly, they can't get it.

Credit often is extended on simple faith and trust. This places the burden of responsibility on each person not to abuse that privilege. People who abuse credit hurt not only themselves, but other people as well. A person who does not repay as promised costs everyone else extra in the form of both higher prices of goods and higher interest rates.

## The Advantages of Having and Using Good Credit

The principal advantage of credit is that it enables you to get what you want or need without having to wait while saving the entire price. Not having to wait can be really important when, for example, an emergency arises. In times of emergency, a person without good credit can be in a real jam. Sometimes the best thing about having good credit is just knowing that it is there if and when needed.

*Good Credit Is an Advantage When Disaster Strikes*

Of course, a person can survive without using credit. In fact, some people have no choice. They have to get by without credit because no one will grant it to them because they are considered a poor risk. All other things being equal, if you manage your income intelligently using credit, you will accomplish much more than a person who has to manage the same income *without* using any form of credit.

A good credit rating also could mean the difference between whether or not you get a particular job you may apply for one day. Employers often get a credit report on job applicants. Why? They want someone who is financially stable and uses good judgment.

Again, one of the most important reasons for having good credit is just plain having it. There is the fantastic feeling of pride and sense of accomplishment in having a good reputation and the security that goes with it. This is a sense of well-being that few other things can duplicate. It means that, whether or not you make a lot of money, you keep your word. People know that, and they respect and trust you. And they would be willing to lend money to you.

### How to Start Establishing Your Good Credit

The best time to start your good credit is *before* you need it. Like a lot of other good things in life, that takes preparation — thinking ahead.

Here are a few of the things a creditor looks for in all credit applications. He or she looks even more closely at these things in the case of a young person just starting out.

- *Personal stability.* Age is a part of this, but a creditor also is vitally interested in how mature you behave and appear and in how you represent yourself.

- *Income.* How much do you earn, and how stable is that income? How long have your been employed? Do you earn enough to support the credit you want?

- *Assets.* Do you own anything of value?

- *Savings.* Have you demonstrated a savings habit by gradually building up some savings?

- *What is the credit for?* Is the purpose of the credit sensible and prudent?

- *Are you making a reasonable down payment,* or can you put up collateral? Let's say you want to buy a used car costing $2,500, and you have saved a $500 down payment. That's a lot more attractive deal to a creditor than the guy who wants a new Z-28 and has "zip" for a down payment.

If you fall a little short of some of these items (and most young people do), the creditor may tell you that you need a co-signer. A co-signer is another person who promises to pay the creditor if you don't. This business of co-signing is so important that a whole section on that topic follows later.

Start developing your good reputation before you have to use it. A record of good, responsible behavior will pave the way to getting credit later.

Here are some suggestions that you can use to build good credit quickly:

1.  Start a savings habit. If you have savings (and if you're over 18), you can borrow using your savings as collateral.

2.  Never bounce checks when you have a checking account. The way you handle your checking account becomes part of your credit record.

3.  Never apply for credit just to see if you can get it. That's not wise, and it can hurt you.

4.  Be sensible in what credit you start, and pay exactly as agreed. As you start to get a little credit, be patient and don't try for too much too soon.

In time, you will have built a strong record. Keep it that way! Next time you borrow five bucks from Mom or Dad or a friend, remember your credit is at stake.

Chuck used those tips to start his credit. By the time he was 18, he had savings from his part-time job. He made a loan against those savings, paid it back quickly, and that started his credit. The loan officer remembered him later and was impressed with him.

*Evidence of Chuck's Financial Responsibility*
*Impressed the Loan Officer*

In recent years, there has been a trend to make credit more available to young people. As but one example, credit card companies often send pre-approved credit applications to college students. Lenders have learned that college students, for the most part, will be responsible credit users. Most college students have not yet established favorable credit ratings. But the credit card issuers take some risk, believing that many of these students will become good customers for life.

Another recent trend is the development of "secured" credit cards. This is where a credit card company will provide a credit card to someone who has not established good credit, or maybe even has some blemishes on his or her credit record. But this line of credit must be secured by a saving account! So, you must put up your own savings as security, and you cannot use your savings while the credit line is active. Seldom are these credit lines at the most favorable rates and terms.

## All About Co-signing

Not every young person is as fortunate as Chuck. In fact, many don't have some of the good things going for them that Chuck did. Even if you are a bit short on some of the factors that a creditor looks at, you may still be able to start your credit with the help of a co-signer. One day, someone may even ask you to co-sign for him or her. You need to learn now what this business of co-signing is all about.

The terms co-signer, co-maker, endorser, and guarantor all mean about the same thing for our purposes. You and the co-signer both sign a note, which is a promise to pay on specific terms. Then *both* you and the co-signer are jointly *and* individually responsible to the creditor for the terms of the note. This means that, if you don't pay for whatever reason, the creditor is going to go after the co-signer. There are no excuses, ifs, ands, or buts. It's that simple.

Co-signing is an excellent means of helping someone start building good credit. But we are here to tell you that it is serious business. You can get Mom, Dad, or whoever co-signed with you all messed up if you are not responsible and mature enough to know what you are doing. Sometimes problems over a co-signed debt cause serious trouble between friends or family members. At worst, these problems can result in financial disaster.

Before you ask someone to co-sign for you, you should first look in the mirror. Would you co-sign for yourself? Do you have your feet on the ground? Is your income stable enough for you to be sure that you can pay back the debt? If it's a bad deal, asking someone to co-sign is a "bummer."

Next, you better hope Mom, Dad, or other co-signer has good credit. If not, their endorsement would be rejected. You see, if they don't have a good record of paying their own debts, why should a creditor believe they will pay your debt if need be?

But there is another problem here, a real sleeper! And we are telling you something a lot of moms and dads may not know. When someone co-signs for someone else, he or she is using some of his or her own credit capacity. In other words, co-signers are expected to be fully able to pay their own bills and have room left over to pay yours, too, if it should become necessary. If Mom and Dad have their hands full financially trying to keep you fed and in designer jeans, they might not be able to co-sign for that car you want. All people, no matter how high their income, have limits on how much they can borrow. There's no exact formula, but there is a limit. That's something we tell you a little more about next.

## How Much Can You Borrow?

As we mentioned earlier, how much credit a person can stand depends on several things. Remember the three Cs — Character, Capacity, and Capital. There is no exact way these three things can be measured. Also, life has a way of throwing curve balls at you. Your income may drop. Your expenses may increase. Things you own (which can be used as collateral) may increase or decrease in value. The trick in using credit wisely and staying out of trouble is simply not to overdo it.

Earlier we discussed budgeting. This is simply sitting down and putting a paper and pencil to work. A budget is made up of three simple factors: income, expenses, and obligations. Expenses and obligations must never exceed income, *with a safety factor built in.* Otherwise a person is in trouble.

Income is the money that you can count on coming in from all sources. Expenses are things like food, housing, utilities, gas, and all sorts of other things for which people must have money. Obligations are those things for which you are already committed, such as other debts owed to a bank or department store. If your expected income is far more than the amount you expect to spend plus payments on your obligations, you may have some borrowing capacity.

Sometimes borrowing capacity also depends on other things. If your job is viewed as extremely stable, your credit capacity may be larger than that of someone with the same income but from a job that may not be so certain. The creditor wants to know that you will continue receiving that income.

Often a person with stable income, excellent credit, and assets that have been accumulated over a period of time will have a large borrowing capacity. Often he or she can borrow relatively large sums without even putting up collateral. Wise is the person who has accomplished this. Such a person often has access to borrowing at lower interest rates and on better terms. This is fair, because he or she can demonstrate to the creditor that not much risk would be involved in giving him or her a loan.

To sum all of this up, each person is responsible for knowing how much debt he or she can handle. A little simple budgeting and sometimes a balance sheet are tools that a person can use to make sure that he or she doesn't bite off more than can be chewed. The time to check your credit capacity is before you get into credit trouble!

*Use Credit Carefully to Avoid a Sea of Debt*

## The Balance Sheet

Along with a budget, a "balance sheet" or a "net worth statement" is useful in determining how much you can borrow.

A balance sheet is really a snapshot of a person's financial condition as of a specific date. It has three parts. We've reproduced an example of a balance sheet for you. A balance sheet is often called a "Net Worth Statement."

### Example of a Simple Balance Sheet

| Assets (Things You Own) | | Liabilities (What You Owe) | |
|---|---|---|---|
| Automobile | $2,000 | Auto Loan | $1,500 |
| Sound System | 800 | Mom & Dad | 500 |
| Jewelry | 200 | Charge Account | 300 |
| Savings | 500 | Total Liabilities | $2,300 |
| Checking Account | 300 | | |
| Furniture | 1,000 | Net Worth | 2,500 |
| | | Total Liabilities | |
| Total Assets | $4,800 | And Net Worth | $4,800 |

On the left side of the page is the section called *Assets*. Assets are what you own, even if you owe money on them. On the right side of the statement there are two parts. The first is called *Liabilities*. Liabilities are what you owe on debts and other obligations. The second part on the right side is your *Net Worth*, or *Equity*. That's the difference between what you *own* in the assets section and what you *owe* in the liabilities section. In other words, your liabilities plus your net worth on the right must equal your total assets on the other side. That's why it's called a "Balance Sheet." Both sides have to equal, or be in "balance."

You need not worry too much about making up balance sheets at this point in your life. Later you will have to if you ever apply for some serious credit. You will want to see your net worth increase each year as you make sure that your assets increase faster than your liabilities.

We recommend that every adult stop every so often and make an accounting of his or her financial accomplishments. Once a year is good enough for most folks. This financial accounting, in essence, will be a balance sheet. Just as in the case of the balance sheet of a large corporation, such a General Motors, your balance sheet will include a listing of liabilities (debts), assets (cash and property of value), and the difference will represent your equity, or "Net Worth."

## How to Make Your Own Balance Sheet

First, simply list everything of any significant value that you own. Doing this exercise helps you to remember things that you might otherwise forget. Don't forget that money in your checking or savings account is an asset. If anyone owes you money, then that is an asset too, as long as you know that person will pay you back.

Next, assign your best knowledge of the fair market value to each thing on your list. Fair market value is what something is really worth today, not what you paid for it. A rule of thumb: things like appliances and furniture are now worth about half of what you paid for them, as long as the items are in excellent condition. (For a business, assets are listed at their actual cost less depreciation, not some estimate of current value.)

Then list the current balance of every debt you owe. Do not overlook any kind of debt you have.

Now you can organize the items into a balance sheet. List assets on the left and liabilities on the right. Add each column. We hope the total of your *Assets* will exceed the total of your *Liabilities*. If so, the difference between the two items will be a positive *Net Worth*. This tells you that you are beginning to accumulate wealth. If your liabilities exceed your assets, then you have a negative net worth. That can imply that your past income has not been spent wisely or that you have too many debts. In either case, your financial condition needs some attention — fast.

## All That Glitters

As good as credit is, it's not gold. It's a powerful tool and can bite the hand that doesn't treat it with respect. Handled with care, credit can improve your lifestyle and your sense of self-respect. It can help you in an emergency. However, it is not to be abused.

In the first place, remember that good credit does not increase your income. It doesn't magically make you able to afford things beyond your ability to produce an income to pay for them. While credit can make buying things much easier, it still won't enable you to keep up with the Joneses if they make a lot more money than you do!

In addition, sometimes credit can increase temptation too much. If you are too impulsive and can't say no to yourself, good credit can be your worst enemy. Of course, it wouldn't be for long. If you mess things up too badly, you won't have that good credit very long!

*Take Care of Your Credit — Stop and*
*Think Before You Spend*

Credit can be addictive. Weak or impulsive people can get hooked on credit to the point of financial self-destruction. It's just like getting hooked on drugs or alcohol. The ones who think they are too tough or too smart usually are the ones who stupidly find themselves in trouble.

Credit cannot replace the need for savings. There is a time to use credit and a time to pay cash. Don't use credit too frequently and for things for which credit was never intended. It can make you forget that savings are a critical part of your financial life. Then one day you find you have become too dependent on credit. You are caught in a vicious cycle that isn't easily broken.

Some people use a credit card for everyday, routine purchases, but they pay the balance in full each month. That's using credit for convenience. That is fine as long as the individual is a good manager and limits total monthly charges to an amount he or she can pay.

Used intelligently, the advantages of credit almost always outweigh the interest cost. But if you abuse credit and use it poorly, you could find the interest cost consuming a lot of the income you earn. Then you are in a bad situation.

Believe it or not, some people simply should never use credit. They just can't "hack it." It's just like pouring gas on a fire. They will repeatedly get themselves into trouble. These really are not bad people; their skills just lie elsewhere!

Most people will agree that the intelligent use of credit carries more reward than price. But, remember that when you use credit, you are spending your future income — all the more reason to learn how to make wise decisions.

Use credit wisely to gain benefits. Beware of credit abuse. Sometimes you just have to say "no" to yourself and to too much borrowing.

## What if Trouble Strikes?

There is risk in everything. Nobody really knows what the future holds. We control most of what happens to us by using good judgment and common sense. There are so many uncertainties in life that it can boggle your mind. Will you have a date for the party Saturday night? Will you fall in love? Will you go to college? Will you get a good job? All of these uncertainties and more face each of us every day. We wish we could tell you that uncertainty would one day vanish from your life. But we cannot do that.

What does this have to do with money and credit? A lot! Very few people are going to get out of this life without facing one or more financial crisis. In this section, we tell you some of the things you can do when trouble strikes.

Unexpected illness, loss of a job through no fault of your own, or any other of a number of things can cause financial problems. When adverse circumstances strike, it won't do any good to feel sorry for yourself. You simply have to look for the positive things you can do. You have to make things better.

The first step in dealing with financial trouble is to recognize it quickly. Accept that it's really facing you and that you must do something. You will always have choices, and the worst choice is to stick your head in the sand and ignore the problem. That won't work. The problem will not go away by itself.

Once you accept your problem, you must look around for the choices that are open. You always have choices that can make things better, even if some are painful. List your options, using common sense to think each one through.

If the problem is a loss of income, you must do everything possible to replace that income as quickly as you can. Waiting for a good job to come find *you* just won't cut it. But that's what some people do! You usually should take the first honest job you can get that produces income. It is often easier to get a better job when you are working than it is to find work when you're unemployed.

If the problem is that you've simply used too much credit, you must stop using credit until some of the debt is paid off. This is where a lot of people go wrong. They don't want to face how much they owe. So they keep on using credit, waiting for a raise or a promotion to bail them out. And they sink deeper into debt.

If bills come due and you can't pay them right then, sit down and take stock. Make a plan to get back on track. Call each creditor that you owe and explain the problem. If you can show creditors that you have a plan to deal with your situation, they usually are more than happy to help. If you don't call them first, they're going to call you. Then they aren't going to be as pleasant to deal with!

If the problems are too serious for you to handle alone, call a professional. There are over 1,200 non-profit Consumer Credit Counseling Service office locations in the country. They have experts to help people deal with credit problems. These services are supported by creditors concerned with helping a sincere customer who is in trouble. The CCCS headquartered in Baton Rouge operates offices in Alexandria, Bossier City, Gonzales, Hammond, Lafayette, Lake Charles, Marksville, Monroe, Natchitoches, New Iberia, Oakdale, Opelousas, Ruston, Shreveport, Zachary, and El Dorado, Arkansas. Our phone number in the Baton Rouge area is 927-4274. Statewide, we may be reached toll-free at 800-850-CCCS. There is a separate CCCS that serves the New Orleans area. So, in Louisiana, there is help available in every major city and even in smaller communities.

If you are a reader outside of Louisiana, check the white pages of your phone book under Consumer Credit Counseling Service. If you do not see a listing, call 800-388-CCCS. This is a national referral line that will get you in touch with the nearest CCCS office. Watch out for unscrupulous, so-called "counseling" businesses that can really mess up a person. You should always check with your Better Business Bureau or with one or more of your creditors before seeking help from a questionable source.

In Appendix C and Appendix D you will find more complete information on Consumer Credit Counseling Services and Better Business Bureaus.

*CCCS Agencies Can Help With Debt Problems*

## THINGS TO REMEMBER

Credit is created when someone gives you something of value in exchange for your promise to pay at some time in the future.

The time to establish good credit is before you actually need it.

The main advantage of credit is that you can get what you want or need without first having to save the entire purchase price.

Another great advantage of credit is simply the convenience of being able to use it.

A co-signer can help you to start building good credit.

Co-signing a loan is serious business.

An individual should look at his or her financial condition on a regular basis.

Wise use of credit can help you raise your standard of living. Misuse can lead to serious financial problems.

When people get into serious financial trouble, there are non-profit services that can help them.

# Chapter Eight

# Where To Borrow Money

The last chapter covered credit—how to use it and how to avoid abusing it. In this and the following chapter, we tell you how to borrow, where to seek loans, and how to apply for credit.

Chuck Taylor could have waited to buy his car until he had saved up the entire price. But he had good credit and enough income to be able to borrow some of the money he needed. By saving his down payment, he had proved both that he had good self-discipline and that he had adequate disposable income to handle credit payments. Because Chuck had a legitimate need for an automobile, had saved a down payment, and had the income with which to safely make the monthly payments, his financing an automobile was a good example of the wise use of credit.

When Chuck was ready to borrow money, he had to figure out where to go for a loan. There are many willing lenders eager to do business with responsible customers. Choosing one seemed to be a bit complicated, and Chuck wanted to make a good choice; so he took the time to learn about the different types of financial institutions.

## Financial Institutions

Much of the borrowing, use of credit cards, and most of the saving that you do will involve financial institutions. Unless you plan on never having a job, never making a dime, and never owning anything, you, like Chuck, better know something about financial institutions. All through life you'll be doing business with people who *do* know about those things. You don't want to end up with the short end of the stick.

There are three basic types of financial institutions with which most people do business during their life. We mention each briefly below; then we describe in more detail what they can do for you.

**Many Services Are Provided by Financial Institutions**

*Depository institutions.* These are institutions in which you can deposit your money in a savings or checking account and withdraw it pretty much as you wish. These are usually "full-service" institutions, which can make loans and issue credit cards. They can take care of most financial needs that people have. Examples are commercial banks, credit unions, and savings and loan associations.

*Contractual institutions.* Insurance companies and pension funds fall in this category. You make payments to these institutions over a long period of time. You can get your money out only when a particular event occurs. That event could be your death or your retirement.

*Entrepreneurial institutions.* These companies don't take deposits from customers to get their money. They borrow the money elsewhere and then lend it to you. The best example of this type is a consumer finance company.

## Depository Institutions

There are four major types of depository institutions in the United States — commercial banks, savings and loans associations, credit unions, and money market funds. These are very important to most everyone because they serve us in so many ways.

### Commercial Banks

The most important type of depository institution is a commercial bank. More people do business with commercial banks than with any other type of institution. You can find just about any financial service you want. There are about 10,000 commercial banks in the country, and they operate over 55,000 branch locations. The total assets of all banks combined is over $4.1 trillion.

A lot of folks don't know it, but commercial banks are owned by people just like you. Banks issue shares of stock to the owners in exchange for the investment that the owners originally made. Bank stock has value and pays dividends according to the profits the bank makes. Therefore, banks are very much like other businesses, such as Texaco Corporation, General Electric, or Ford Motor Company. They exist to make money for their owners. Banks attempt to offer services that you need and are willing to pay for. They must generate income that exceeds expenses. That's the only way to make a profit.

Banks are very important to us. They accept deposits from the general public. Because of this, they are heavily regulated and supervised by the government. The objective of bank regulation is to make sure that banks are operated in a safe and sound manner so that the money you may have on deposit will be safe. Also, there are regulations to ensure that services are offered with no discrimination on the basis of age, sex, race, religion, or creed.

Your deposit in a commercial bank in the United States is insured up to $100,000 by an agency of the federal government. That agency is the Federal Deposit Insurance Corporation. Commercial banks pay a fee every year to the FDIC. Then, if a bank gets into financial trouble and becomes unable to pay its depositors, the FDIC will arrange for some other bank to take over the deposits or the FDIC will close the bank.

Because the FDIC insures deposits, Congress assumes the right to regulate banks. In fact, banks are perhaps the most heavily regulated business firms in the nation. The cost of that regulation, of course, is passed on to consumers in the form of higher prices.

Among the many services a bank offers are checking accounts, savings accounts of all kinds, financing for cars and other things, credit cards, installment loans, cashier's checks, home mortgages, business loans, trust services, safety deposit boxes, 24-hour ATMs (Automated Teller Machines), and many more.

You need to establish a good banking relationship as soon as you can. In fact, it's not too early to do that now! Even if you are too young to use many of the services a bank offers, you can open a savings account at any age. Later, when you need more of the services offered by a bank, at least you will have already established a banking relationship.

### Credit Unions

These rapidly-growing institutions are "cooperatives." That means they exist for the mutual benefit of their members, who are also owners of the credit union. Members may make deposits just like at a bank. They may also receive loans from their credit union provided they have good credit. While the typical credit union is very small, there are many large ones.

There are more than 12,000 credit unions across the country. In Louisiana alone, there are over 300 credit unions. These credit unions serve over 850,000 members in Louisiana and almost 67 million across the United States. Altogether, credit union members have approximately $260 billion in savings with credit unions.

Credit unions have to make a profit just like any other business. If a credit union's income for a period of time is not greater than its expenses, the credit union cannot build up its capital. Credit unions need capital to protect the deposits of their members from loss which could arise in the course of making loans to members who do not repay.

Most of the larger credit unions offer many services similar to those offered by banks and savings and loan associations. They finance cars and make personal loans; some even make loans for homes and can issue credit cards. Almost all offer what are called "share-draft accounts," which are just like checking accounts at banks.

At about 90 percent of the credit unions, savings up to $100,000 per depositor are insured by the National Credit Union Share Insurance Fund. All federal credit unions are insured by NCUSIF, and most state-chartered ones are as well. So, if an insured credit union gets into financial trouble, savers will be protected by that insurance. Like banks, credit unions pay a premium each year for that insurance. Also like banks, credit unions are closely regulated.

Most credit unions have somewhat restricted membership. Originally, credit unions were established for very small groups, such as employees of a particular company. In recent years, however, memberships are being extended to a much broader base of people. Most credit unions today will allow a relative of a member to be a member!

To join a credit union where you may someday work, all you usually have to do is make a small deposit. Then you are a full member. That entitles you to all the services the credit union offers. Remember, though, to qualify for a loan, you must still be able to demonstrate the "three Cs." In most credit unions, regular payroll deductions are arranged for any amount you wish to save. If you have a large enough balance in your account, you may use it as collateral for a loan, often resulting in a lower interest rate for you. Payments on loans made through credit unions are most often made through payroll deductions. That is, the payment is taken out of the member's paycheck before he or she gets the check.

Payroll deduction can be deceptive for some people. A debt owed to a credit union where you work is still a debt. It is the same as if it were owed to a bank or any other creditor. Some people who tend to twist their thinking to suit their own desires may tell themselves, "Well, that's taken out of my check, so I don't have to worry about it." That can be dangerous thinking. You only have so much credit capacity. It doesn't matter to whom you owe the money, it's a debt. And it must be repaid.

*Savings and Loan Associations*

These companies began many years ago as special purpose institutions. Their business originally involved only one goal — providing credit to enable people to buy homes. Of course, to get the money to lend for home mortgages, S&Ls also accepted deposits from savers. Savings and loans grew very rapidly from the early 1950s until the mid-1980s.

In the 1980s, some government regulations, which limited what these institutions could do, were removed. Some S&Ls branched out into things new to them and to their managements. A large number of S&Ls got into trouble and failed. Many others got caught in a squeeze because their money was loaned out on long-term, low-interest home mortgages at a time when the rates they had to pay to attract deposits rose. Since the mid-1980s, the number of S&Ls has decreased sharply.

S&Ls, like banks, are insured by the full faith and credit of the federal government. All depositors are protected up to the $100,000 limit. So, if your savings are less than that amount and in an S&L, your money is as safe as if it were in a bank.

Today, most S&Ls offer many of the services that banks do.

### Money Market Mutual Funds

If this book had been written before 1980, there would be nothing in it about money market mutual funds. That's because, for all practical purposes, they didn't exist! Today, however, many people hold some of their money in these funds. MMMFs are depository types of institutions, and you can actually write checks against your balance.

Usually the interest rate paid on MMMF deposits exceeds that paid by other institutions, but these funds are not regulated very much. Also, they are not insured by any agency of the federal government. Many are very safe and well managed, but there are so many that you cannot easily get information about all of them. However, they do represent an alternative place for people to deposit some excess money and earn a higher rate. Remember that higher interest usually involves higher risk.

Don't go to a money market mutual fund company and ask for a loan—they will laugh you right out of the place!

### Contractual Financial Institutions

Earlier, we defined these institutions as those in which you put money over a period of time. When a particular event occurs, you get your money back, including some interest or other gain. The two major types of these are pension funds and life insurance companies.

In the case of life insurance, each month or each year you make a payment called a premium. The insurance company takes these premiums paid in by all of their policyholders and invests that money. Depending on the terms of the policy, you get an agreed amount of money back at some future age or your beneficiary gets it when you die.

You may not be thinking about retirement now, but one day you really *will* be concerned about it. Probably your ability to retire will be related to a pension fund. A pension fund works like a life insurance company does. You or your employer (or both of you) make payments every month or every year into the pension fund. That money is invested. When you retire, you begin to draw out your pension benefits. Usually, those benefits are paid monthly for as long as you live. But this is not always the case, because there are many different kinds of retirement plans and pension funds. By the way, many large banks and some S&Ls have "trust departments" that handle investments for people and pension plans for employers.

This is a good place to mention a benefit that more and more employers are offering. It is called a 401(k) salary deferral plan. The "401(k)" name is simply a reference to the part of the federal tax law that makes this plan legal. In a 401(k) plan, an employee may "defer" before-tax income. Defer means to postpone or delay. In this kind of plan, you are deferring income until some point in the future.

Deferring before-tax income provides the saver an incredible advantage. For you to save money in the regular fashion, you do so with after-tax dollars. In other words, you have to earn, for example, $100 to save $80 — the $20 went to pay income tax. Then you have only $80 working for you and earning interest. But if you can save before-tax dollars, you would have the entire $100 in your account and the entire $100 earning interest for you. Normally you would also have to pay income tax on interest that you earn. But, in a 401(k) plan, not only are you able to save before-tax dollars, but the earnings, or interest, are allowed to grow untaxed also. You cannot escape taxation forever — eventually the tax man cometh. When you draw this money out, usually around retirement, you must pay taxes on it. But even so, this plan is very much to an employee's advantage for two reasons. One, you end up with more money. Two, the tax bite is lower because, at retirement, most people are in a lower tax bracket.

And, there is a real good kicker. Some employers who sponsor this kind of plan will "match" the employee's deferral. That is, the company also will put some of its money into your 401(k) account as an incentive for you to save under that plan. A match does not necessarily mean dollar for dollar. It may be, for example, a 50 percent match. That means that, for every $10 an employee saves, the employer will put up an additional $5. With a match, you really build up some big bucks in your account!

Another factor that makes these plans attractive is how easily and painlessly they can work. If your employer offers the plan, you simply sign up, and the amount you choose is deducted from your pay each payday. If you sign up for $10 each payday, your take-home pay will be reduced by less than $10. How much less depends on your tax bracket. Tax brackets are explained in Chapter 14. This is how the "before-tax" feature works.

To gain the benefit of these plans, there are costs. The gain is the tax savings and the building of your future security. What you give up is the current use of the money that you put into the plan. You can't tap your 401(k) plan any time you need a little extra money. If you draw money from plans like this before age 59½, you have to pay penalties.

Not all employers offer plans like this. So, to help other people save for retirement, the government allows what is called an "IRA." This stands for Individual Retirement Account. Most everyone, except extremely high-income people, can benefit from an IRA. You can open one with a bank or other qualified institution, and deposit up to $2,000 each year. If you are not eligible for a 401(k) or other employer-sponsored retirement plan, you get to deduct this amount from your taxable income when you file your IRS return. The concept is very similar to a 401(k), except it takes more discipline. You have to make the payment into your IRA — it does not automatically come out of your paycheck. The earnings from an IRA are tax-deferred, just as in a 401(k).

We tell you about these things because they are important. And, by getting this far in this book, you have demonstrated the maturity to be able to understand these things and begin to think and plan ahead. That's what financial responsibility is all about. Use of knowledge and information like this is how people accumulate wealth and secure their financial future. Learning about and taking advantage of things like this is what sets some people apart from others.

### Entrepreneurial Financial Institutions

This type of business corporation borrows huge sums of money in the financial markets. In turn, they lend money out in smaller amounts to individuals and sometimes to other businesses. The most common example of this kind of company is a consumer finance or small loan company. These companies do not offer any other service; they just specialize in making relatively small loans to individuals.

Consumer finance companies got started to help fill a need for credit. They continue today as an important source of credit for many people and for many reasons. In some cases, a person may be a good credit risk, but doesn't qualify for a bank loan for one reason or another. In other cases, consumer finance companies may be a little more likely to grant credit to someone who appears to be a greater risk. The small loan company deals with fewer customers and generally knows them better. Also, a small loan company may accept collateral that a bank may not. Many other types of lenders simply will not make small loans involving less than, say, $1,500. So consumer finance companies fill a need in the marketplace.

Most credit granted by a consumer finance company is in the form of "installment" loans. You borrow a specific amount of money, and you pay it back in regular monthly payments for an agreed number of months. This is a good form of credit for people who might tend to overspend with a credit card.

In many cases, the interest rate consumer finance companies charge may be higher than that available from some other sources of credit. But we've already pointed out that they provide loans that are not attractive to many other lenders. All in all, consumer finance companies provide a very valuable service and fill an important need for a lot of people.

Captive automobile finance companies are a kind of entrepreneurial institution. They are associated with and owned by the major automobile manufacturing companies. Examples are Ford Motor Credit Corporation, General Motors Acceptance Corporation, and Chrysler Credit Corporation. If you buy a car, the dealer may try to get you to finance the car through one of these lenders. Like anything else, remember to shop around for the best deal on your auto loan.

Chuck Taylor checked out several financial institutions. He ended up borrowing from the place where he had his savings account, which he had started years ago. These people knew him and had treated him well, and he got a relatively low interest rate on his loan.

## THINGS TO REMEMBER

The three basic types of financial institutions are depository institutions, contractual institutions, and entrepreneurial institutions.

Banks, credit unions, and savings and loan associations are important depository institutions.

Insurance companies and pension funds are the main types of contractual institutions.

Consumer finance companies are entrepreneurial institutions. They provide a specialized service, often willing to make smaller loans than other institutions.

## Chapter Nine

# Borrowing From a Financial Institution

Selecting a financial institution was only Chuck's first step in getting a car loan. There was more for him to learn and understand before he got the loan. Some things he had heard about before, but much was new to him. After reading this, you'll be way ahead of where Chuck was back then.

Borrowing money usually is simple for people who are established and have good credit. We've already told you how to start your credit. There are, however, some important things that you, Chuck, or any borrower needs to understand. Let's look at some of these things.

*What's Involved in Making a Loan?*

## Interest Rates

When financial institutions extend credit, they expect to be rewarded! That reward is profit. Not only do they expect the money they lend to be repaid, but they must charge interest for the use of the money. The interest they collect is their income. It must cover all expenses plus produce a profit. Among their expenses is the cost to them of the money they lend. Another type of expense is the losses they incur when some people don't pay them back. When someone skips out or takes bankruptcy, lenders pass that cost on to other borrowers in the form of higher interest rates.

The amount of interest we pay to borrow money depends on two things: (1) the interest rate and (2) the period of time we have use of the money. Let's look first at the interest rate.

There is a federal law called the "Truth in Lending Act." Among other things, that law requires all lenders to express the interest rate in terms of "APR," or Annual Percentage Rate. We're not going to bore you with the math of how that rate is calculated. The important thing is that all lenders must calculate the interest rate the same way, so that you can compare rates charged by different lenders.

While it's a good idea to compare interest rates, you may not always want to borrow from the cheapest source. There are other factors which can be very important. For example, you may have a good relationship with a certain institution. That relationship can be very valuable, as Chuck found out. The people at that institution know you, and you know them. Finding a good lender and sticking with him or her can be very important to you. Of course, if the rates are way out of line compared to those offered by other lenders, that's another matter. If possible, however, you should stick with one lender and build a good relationship over a long time. The lender will value your good business and will compete to keep that business.

Remember, the better your credit is, the more valuable your business is to a lender — also, the more likely you are to get a lower interest rate.

There are other factors that affect interest rates in general. Inflation, for example, is one. If we are in a period in which prices are rising, interest rates can be expected to rise also. If a lot of people and businesses are borrowing a lot of money, loan demand is high. Interest rates will also tend to increase. Remember, interest is the price of money and credit. The supply and demand factors described in Chapter Three apply to credit as well as other things.

## Other Costs of Borrowing

### *Insurance*

There will often be other costs in addition to interest. Most lenders will offer to sell you a "credit life" insurance policy. That way the lender will be repaid by the insurance company in the event of your death. In some states, credit life insurance may be optional. In other states, the lender may require that it be purchased. If you agree to purchase this insurance, the lender will offer to include the premium in the amount you finance.

If you are financing an automobile, you may be required to buy property insurance, such as collision and comprehensive, to protect the collateral. When you obtain a mortgage for a home, the lender will require you to purchase property insurance. When Chuck financed his car, he had to purchase insurance to cover theft or damage to the car in the event he had an accident.

It is important that you learn about the different types of insurance. In the last paragraph, we briefly mentioned collision and comprehensive insurance. Nearly every state requires by law that you purchase liability coverage, but that is a totally different type of insurance. Make sure you study Chapter 12, which covers the basics of insurance.

If the lender requires that insurance be purchased, remember that you are not required to buy the insurance from the lender. You may obtain acceptable coverage from whatever source you wish. So, shop around for the lowest cost.

## Penalties

If you do not pay an obligation as agreed, you can count on there being some stiff penalties for late payments. If you get behind on your payments, it will cost you money, and it will affect your credit rating. If you really get into trouble with a debt, you may be sued. This can add attorney fees and court costs to what you must pay.

## Other Costs

There may be other costs and fees, but the law requires that these be disclosed to you when you borrow money. When you make a loan, the lender is required by law to provide you a *Disclosure Statement*. This shows you all costs of the transaction, including the interest rate. Most state laws will permit some sort of one-time charge by the lender for setting up the loan. This and any other charges will be revealed on the "Disclosure Statement."

### Term, or Maturity of the Loan

Often other terms can be as important as the APR, or interest rate. The faster you pay back the money, all other things being equal, the less is your interest cost. You may be attracted to small monthly payments, but this arrangement can be costly. Not only will you end up paying back more dollars, but you will be paying for a longer period of time. Making payments each month gets old. But there is another important factor here. Remember credit capacity? The faster you pay a debt back, the faster you regain that amount of your credit capacity. In practical terms, it can mean that you can use your credit again sooner to buy something else.

Most consumer-type loans are repaid in installments. You pay a set amount each month for a given number of months.

This is the most convenient way to repay for most people, but there can be other ways.

In contrast to the installment loan, there is the term loan. With a term loan, the borrower pays back the loan in full all at once at the end of the agreed time. This time can be for any period agreed upon, but most often is 90 days. At the end of that time, the principal (amount borrowed) and the interest must be repaid. Often the lender will agree beforehand that you may pay only the interest due and sign a new note for another 90 days — that is, if you maintain your good credit.

## Collateral

As long as your credit is excellent and the amount of credit you want is not excessive, you may get a loan on your "signature." In that case, you need no collateral. But usually a lender requires that you pledge certain assets (something of value that you own) as security or collateral for your loan. So another factor that you will consider in making a loan is the collateral requirement.

When you buy something expensive on credit, that item almost always becomes collateral. When Chuck bought his new car, a mortgage was recorded in favor of the lender. That means that, until the loan is repaid, the car is pledged as security. There's a minor detail worth mentioning here. When you mortgage something, you cannot sell that property without first paying the debt owed. Until Chuck's car is paid for, he can't sell it without making arrangements with the lender. He might trade the car in before it is fully paid for. When he does, he will have to arrange to add the balance he owes to the amount of the new loan. That may be okay as long as Chuck has built up what is called "equity" in his automobile. For there to be equity, the car must be worth more than the amount still owed on the mortgage.

Many young people finance their first new car for a very long term. This is in an attempt to get their monthly payments low, and partly because they may not have a large down payment. Then, before they have paid long enough to build up equity, they get tired of that car and want another. They may find out that the value of the car is less than the amount they still owe.

## Making the Loan

After a person has established good credit and a relationship with a particular bank, S&L, credit union, or finance company, all it usually takes is a simple phone call to request a loan. Everything can be arranged in advance. All that would remain is for the borrower to drop by to sign the note and get the money.

Let's hope you've done some of the things we talked about in the section on establishing credit. If you don't have any credit or savings, have only three months on a shaky job, and have no co-signer, forget it. But let's assume some other things. First, you're over 18. That's the age of *majority*, which means at least you are legally capable of obligating yourself. Second, you worked part-time during school and have a little money in savings. Third, now you are working full-time, or you may still be living with family while working part-time and in school. In any case, you have *discretionary income*. That means you make enough money to take on a credit obligation.

Think for a few minutes. Who do you want to try to borrow from? Have you ever met anyone who lends money? Who do your family members deal with? Who does your employer deal with? Talk to someone you respect, and you may be referred to a good creditor.

When applying for a loan, prepare yourself by thinking through some questions. What do you want to borrow the money for? Would *you* lend money for that purpose? How much do you really need to borrow? What is it that you want to buy? Have you shopped around? Next, spend a few minutes with paper and pencil and work up a budget. Prepare a list of any existing obligations. All of this only takes a few minutes, and you've accomplished two important things. One, you should now know whether or not you have any business asking for a loan, and two, you are ready to make a good impression.

When you apply for a loan, the lender will ask you some questions. You need to have answers. Make sure you know how much your gross income is and how much your net income (take-home pay) is. Take-home pay is the amount you earned less payroll deductions for things like retirement, insurance, income taxes, and Social Security taxes. There is more about income and Social Security taxes in Chapter 14.

Next, simply call the bank, credit union, S&L, or finance company you've chosen, and tell someone that you would like to come in to discuss a loan. You should take along your paycheck stubs just in case. It wouldn't hurt to take with you a copy of your federal income tax return for last year. When you get there, let's hope you've dressed neatly and have a decent haircut. Remember what we said about eye contact? Simply introduce yourself and go for it!

## The Credit Application

As Chuck knew, you can't just walk into a financial institution, get the money, and walk out! At least not if you haven't already established a good credit relationship with that institution. Your first step is the application for credit. The lender has to know who you are, where you live and work, and a lot of other details. While a credit application may seem intimidating, it's really not. Study the illustrations of a credit application. If you were a lender getting ready to make a loan decision, you would want this information also. Look at the information provided by the two applicants. To whom would you be willing to make a loan?

An important rule: Always be accurate and completely truthful in giving information on a credit application. Never

# APPLICATION FOR LOAN
## MONEYWISE NATIONAL BANK

Please Print

Equal Housing LENDER

You REQUEST AN ADVANCE OF $ 350.00   PURPOSE VCR

## APPLICANT

DRIVER'S LIC. NO. 1068833   STATE LA

| FIRST NAME | INITIAL | LAST NAME | DATE OF BIRTH |
|---|---|---|---|
| WILLIAM | L | SLATER | 9-30-76 |

| SOCIAL SECURITY NO. | MARITAL STATUS | NO. OF DEPENDENTS | HOME TELEPHONE NO. |
|---|---|---|---|
| 480-22-1168 | ☒ Single ☐ Married ☐ Separated | -0- | 555-6651 |

ACTUAL PRESENT RESIDENCE 1020 North STREET   ☒ Rent ☐ Own   MONTHLY PAYMENT $ 225.00

| CITY | STATE | ZIP CODE | COUNTY | YEARS | MONTHS |
|---|---|---|---|---|---|
| ANYWHERE | LA | 70732 | ALLEN | 0 | 3 |

FORMER STREET ADDRESS 214 TEXAS ST.   CITY ANYWHERE   STATE TEXAS   ZIP CODE 22341   YEARS 12   MONTHS 2

PERMANENT STREET ADDRESS Same as above   CITY   STATE   ZIP CODE   YEARS   MONTHS

ARE YOU A CITIZEN OF THE UNITED STATES? ☒ YES ☐ NO   IF NOT, DO YOU HAVE PERMANENT RESIDENCE STATUS? ☐ YES ☐ NO   PERMANENT RESIDENCY NO.

NAME OF NEAREST RELATIVE NOT LIVING WITH YOU   NAME LOUIS M. SLATER   STREET ADDRESS ANYWHERE   CITY TEXAS   STATE/ZIP 22341   PHONE   RELATIONSHIP FATHER

## OCCUPATION

TIME EMPLOYED

CURRENT EMPLOYER (IF SELF-EMPLOYED, LIST COMPANY INCOME VERIFICATION REQUIRED) JOSEPH JOHNSON   POSITION STOCK CLERK   YEARS -   MONTHS 8

BUSINESS STREET ADDRESS 8861 GROVE BLVD.   CITY ANYWHERE   STATE LA   ZIP CODE 70832   BUSINESS PHONE 555-9134

PREVIOUS EMPLOYER   ADDRESS   POSITION   YEARS   MONTHS

### JOB INCOME (MONTHLY NET)

SOURCES OF ADDITIONAL INCOME (FOR EXAMPLE, STOCKS, REAL ESTATE, RETIREMENT, ETC.)

Child support, alimony, or separate maintenance income need not be revealed unless you wish to have it considered as a basis for repaying this obligation.

| | | | |
|---|---|---|---|
| APPLICANT $ 300.00 | SOURCE: PARENT | AMOUNT: $ 200.00 | |
| CO-APPLICANT $ | SOURCE: | AMOUNT: $ | |
| TOTAL $ 300.00 | SOURCE: | AMOUNT: $ | |

## COMPLETE FOR JOINT APPLICATION

| | NAME | DATE OF BIRTH | RELATIONSHIP |
|---|---|---|---|
| SOCIAL SECURITY NO. | DRIVERS LIC. NO. | STATE | EMPLOYER | POSITION | BUSINESS PHONE | YEARS | MONTHS |

## CREDIT REFERENCES

PLEASE LIST ALL YOUR DEBTS. LIST CREDIT UNIONS, BANKS, FINANCE COMPANIES, DEPARTMENT STORE REFERENCES (OPEN)

| Creditor Name/Address & Account No./Collateral | Monthly Payment | Balance Owed | Pay-Off Balance |
|---|---|---|---|
| | | | |
| | | | |
| | | | |
| | | | |
| | | | |
| | | | |
| | | | |
| TOTAL $ | | | |

IN THE LAST 10 YEARS HAVE YOU DECLARED BANKRUPTCY OR FILED A PETITION FOR CHAPTER 13?   Y   N ✓

HAVE YOU HAD PROPERTY FORECLOSED UPON OR GIVEN TITLE OR DEED IN LIEU THEREOF IN THE LAST 7 YEARS?   Y   N

### PERSONAL FINANCIAL STATEMENT

| Assets | | Value | | pmt/month | balance | date opened |
|---|---|---|---|---|---|---|
| Checking Acct. (Bank) | CITIZENS | $ 100.00 | House Pmt/Rent | $ 225.00 | $ | |
| Savings Acct. (Bank) | CITIZENS | $ 300.00 | Co.: | | | |
| Savings Acct. (Bank) | | $ | Auto Pmt. | $ | $ | |
| Stock/Bonds (itemize) | | $ | Co.: | | | |
| Life Ins. Cash Value | | $ | Credit Cards | $ | $ | |
| | | $ | Co.: | | | |
| Household Goods (estimate) | | $ | Insurance | $ | $ | |
| Other Assets | Bike | $ 50.00 | Bank Loans | $ | $ | |
| | | $ | | $ | $ | |
| Auto: Year | Make | $ | Other (alimony, child | | | |
| Auto: Year | Make | $ | support, home owners | | | |
| | | | assn., etc.) | $ | | |
| TOTAL ASSETS | | 450.00 | TOTAL LIABILITIES | | 0.00 | |

Liabilities

APPLICANT'S SIGNATURE William L. Slater   DATE 8/1/95   SEAL

APPROVED   YES   NO

# APPLICATION FOR LOAN
## MONEYWISE NATIONAL BANK

Equal Housing
LENDER

**Please Print**

YOU REQUEST AN ADVANCE OF $ **650.00**   PURPOSE **Auto Repairs**

## APPLICANT

| DRIVER'S LIC. NO. | | STATE | |
|---|---|---|---|

FIRST NAME **Mary**   INITIAL **B.**   LAST NAME **Brown**   DATE OF BIRTH **1/10/72**

SOCIAL SECURITY NO. **101-31-6500**

MARITAL STATUS: ☑ Single  ☐ Married  ☐ Separated

NO. OF DEPENDENTS **0**

HOME TELEPHONE NO. **555-5260**

ACTUAL PRESENT RESIDENCE **1015 Pine St.**   ☑ Rent  ☐ Own   MONTHLY PAYMENT $ **300.00**

CITY **Anywhere**   STATE **LA**   ZIP CODE **70733**   COUNTY **Allen**   YEARS **2**   MONTHS **3**

FORMER STREET ADDRESS **3655 4th St.**   CITY **Anywhere**   STATE **GA**   ZIP CODE **82331**   YEARS **15**   MONTHS **0**

PERMANENT STREET ADDRESS **1015 Pine Ave.**   CITY **Anywhere**   STATE **LA**   ZIP CODE **70733**   YEARS   MONTHS

ARE YOU A CITIZEN OF THE UNITED STATES? ☑ YES  ☐ NO   IF NOT, DO YOU HAVE PERMANENT RESIDENCE STATUS? ☐ YES  ☐ NO   PERMANENT RESIDENCY NO.

NAME OF NEAREST RELATIVE NOT LIVING WITH YOU   NAME **Susan Jones**   STREET ADDRESS **411 Iron**   CITY **Anywhere**   STATE/ZIP **GA**   PHONE **555-8866**   RELATIONSHIP **Sister**

## OCCUPATION

TIME EMPLOYED

CURRENT EMPLOYER (IF SELF-EMPLOYED, LIST COMPANY INCOME VERIFICATION REQUIRED) **Sam's Wholesale**   POSITION **Secretary**   YEARS **1**   MONTHS **11**

BUSINESS STREET ADDRESS **911 South Blvd.**   CITY **Anywhere**   STATE **LA**   ZIP CODE **70733**   BUSINESS PHONE **555-1163**

PREVIOUS EMPLOYER **ABC Cleaners**   ADDRESS **Anywhere, LA**   POSITION **Cashier**   YEARS **2**   MONTHS **4**

JOB INCOME (MONTHLY NET)

SOURCES OF ADDITIONAL INCOME (FOR EXAMPLE, STOCKS, REAL ESTATE, RETIREMENT, ETC.) Child support, alimony, or separate maintenance income need not be revealed unless you wish to have it considered as a basis for repaying this obligation.

| | | | |
|---|---|---|---|
| APPLICANT $ **950.00** | SOURCE: | AMOUNT: $ | |
| CO-APPLICANT $ | SOURCE: | AMOUNT: $ | |
| TOTAL $ **950.00** | SOURCE: | AMOUNT: $ | |

## COMPLETE FOR JOINT APPLICATION

| | NAME | | DATE OF BIRTH | RELATIONSHIP |
|---|---|---|---|---|

| SOCIAL SECURITY NO. | DRIVERS LIC. NO. | STATE | EMPLOYER | POSITION | BUSINESS PHONE | YEARS | MONTHS |
|---|---|---|---|---|---|---|---|

## CREDIT REFERENCES

PLEASE LIST ALL YOUR DEBTS. LIST CREDIT UNIONS, BANKS, FINANCE COMPANIES, DEPARTMENT STORE REFERENCES (OPEN)

| Creditor Name/Address & Account No./Collateral | Monthly Payment | Balance Owed | Pay-Off Balance |
|---|---|---|---|
| Brock's Dept. Store | 75.00 | 225.00 | |
| World Insurance Co. | 84.00 | Monthly | |
| | | | |
| | | | |
| | | | |
| | | | |
| TOTAL $ | 159.00 | | |

IN THE LAST 10 YEARS HAVE YOU DECLARED BANKRUPTCY OR FILED A PETITION FOR CHAPTER 13?  Y ☐  N ☑

HAVE YOU HAD PROPERTY FORECLOSED UPON OR GIVEN TITLE OR DEED IN LIEU THEREOF IN THE LAST 7 YEARS?  Y ☐  N ☐

## PERSONAL FINANCIAL STATEMENT

| Assets | | Value | | Liabilities | pmt/month | balance | date opened |
|---|---|---|---|---|---|---|---|
| Checking Acct. (Bank) | Moneywise Natl. Bank | $ 600.00 | House Pmt/Rent | | $ 300.00 | $ | |
| Savings Acct. (Bank) | Credit Union | $ 1,200.00 | Co.: | | | | |
| Savings Acct. (Bank) | | $ | Auto Pmt. | | $ | $ | |
| Stock/Bonds (itemize) | | $ | Co.: | | | | |
| Life Ins. Cash Value | | $ | Credit Cards | | $ 75.00 | $ 600.00 | |
| | | $ | Co.: | | | | |
| Household Goods (estimate) | | $ 3,000.00 | Insurance | | $ 84.00 | $ | |
| Other Assets | | $ | Bank Loans | | $ | $ | |
| | | $ | Co.: | | $ | $ | |
| Auto: Year **1991** Make **Ford** | | $ 4,000.00 | Other (alimony, child | | | | |
| Auto: Year Make | | $ | support, home owners | | | | |
| | | | assn., etc.) | | $ | | |
| TOTAL ASSETS | | $8,800.00 | TOTAL LIABILITIES | | $600.00 | | |

Everything I have stated in this application is correct to the best of my knowledge. MoneyWise National Bank is authorized to check my credit, employment history, obtain a credit report, and to answer questions about their credit experience with me. I understand that it may be a federal crime punishable by fine or imprisonment, or both, to knowingly make any false statements concerning any of the above facts as applicable under the provisions of the United States Criminal Code.

APPLICANT'S SIGNATURE **Mary B. Brown**   SEAL   DATE **8/1/95**

APPROVED   YES   NO

violate this rule. The application requires your signature, and you are stating that the information is accurate.

After the application is complete, the lender will check your credit rating at one or more credit bureaus. The lender probably will verify your employment and other information you have given. You see, a lender has a great responsibility to control the risk. He or she must make every effort to make good loans. It's not a question of the lender not believing you; the loan officer simply is doing his or her job.

## Types of Loans

There are many different kinds of loans available to individuals. Lenders often call these "products." They design and advertise them to make them attractive. Remember that this is a free market economy, and there is competition for your business. There are car loans, signature loans, consolidation loans, and home mortgage loans, just to name a few. Some institutions make nearly every kind of loan there is. Others aggressively specialize in one or two kinds. A few, like the captive auto finance companies, only make one kind of consumer-type loan. When selecting a lender to apply to for a loan, make sure it offers the kind you need.

### Simple Interest Loans

In this kind of loan, the interest owed on the current balance is calculated each month and subtracted from your payment. The amount left is called a "principal" payment. This is what is subtracted from your balance to determine how much you still owe. All normal home financing is done this way, and many institutions use this method for automobile financing.

In simple interest loans, the amount of interest taken out of payments during the early part of the loan will be higher. This is because the balance is the highest (you owe the creditor more). As you make payments over the life of the loan, the interest drops because you owe less each month.

## Discount Loans

Some loans are "discounted." In such cases, the total amount of interest to be paid for the expected term of the loan is added to the amount you borrow. You sign the note for this amount. It may seem large because it includes what you borrow plus the interest for the time you use the money. As long as you make payments on time, your entire payment is subtracted from the balance. If you pay off a discounted loan in advance, a "rebate" is calculated and subtracted from the gross balance. Because you incur most of the interest expense in the early part of the term when you owe more, the rebate may seem small.

## Short-Term vs. Long-Term Borrowing

The total cost of borrowing depends on a combination of factors. These include interest rate, the term of the loan (maturity), and other costs such as insurance and fees. There is a simple fact that not enough people have learned. The most important way to reduce interest costs when using credit is to repay a debt as quickly as possible. While the interest rate is important, the amount of time you use someone else's money often has a much bigger impact on your cost of using credit.

Study the examples given on the following pages. The first illustrates how you can pay for a home in 15 years for only slightly larger monthly payments than for a 30-year mortgage. The second shows you how much you can save by financing a car for three years instead of for five. While the monthly payments are larger, the savings are great. You will build equity much faster.

We use an assumed interest rate in these examples. In addition, we use what is called "simple interest" calculations. These examples do not include insurance premiums or other charges in the *amount financed*. You learned in this book that you do not have to purchase credit life insurance from the lender as a requirement for a loan. If the loan is for an automobile, a creditor may require that you keep the collateral insured for the life of the mortgage. You can often save money by arranging for the collision and comprehensive insurance on your own.

### Financing a Home

While buying your own home may not be in the cards for you right now, let's start with this example. It involves a "starter" home, maybe not the castle in your dreams.

| | | |
|---|---|---|
| Sales Price ........ | $50,000 | (money going to the seller) |
| Closing Costs...... | $500 | (costs associated with making the loan) |
| Points ........... | $500 | (another cost associated with the loan) |
| Down Payment .... | ($5,000) | (10% of the sales price) |
| Amount Financed .. | $46,000 | (this is what your mortgage will be) |

For a conventional 30-year mortgage at 7.75 percent interest, the monthly payments will be **$329.56**. The same mortgage, but for 15 years, requires monthly payments of **$433.00**.

The monthly payments for half the time are not double! They are only $103.44 more, or 32 percent higher. Now let's look at how much you save by going for the higher payments.

In the case of the 30-year loan, you would make 360 payments (30 years times 12 months). You would pay back a total of $118,641.60 over the term of the loan.

For the 15-year loan, you would make 180 monthly payments (15 times 12). At $433.00 per payment, you would pay back $77,940.00 over the 15-year period.

So, by swallowing the higher payments, you save $40,701.60 ($118,641.60 minus $77,940.00)! Not only that, but your home is paid for in half the time. Moreover, with the shorter loan, you would lower the balance much more quickly and build "equity" faster. You might be able to move up to a nicer home by using that equity.

The example we have given you assumed a 7.75 percent loan. While interest rates will fluctuate over time, in recent years that rate has been fairly typical. In addition, the interest rate on a 15-year loan will always be smaller, other factors being constant. So, the actual saving on the 15-year loan is even greater than our example shows.

Don't let the large payback numbers scare you. If you don't buy a home, you would have to pay rent. So, you would still pay out some big bucks over 15 or 30 years. The interest on a home loan is deductible from your taxable income. This means that you would pay less income tax; so, the monthly payments would be somewhat reduced on an after-tax basis.

## Bi-Weekly Payments

There is still another trick in paying back a mortgage on a home and saving even more money. Some lending institutions will allow you to make half-payments every other week. Such an arrangement works well if you have a job that provides a paycheck every other week. This means you make 26 half-payments in a year, or the equivalent of 13 monthly payments. This will not only build equity faster, but will save even more interest costs. Don't arrange this unless the mortgage also allows you to switch to normal monthly payments if you should ever want to. You may change jobs and start getting paid once a month or on the first and fifteenth.

One more thing about arranging a mortgage. Even if you agree to the longer mortgage, make sure it allows you to make extra payments on the principal without penalty. Then you can voluntarily make larger or extra payments to reduce the balance and save interest costs. If you commit to the shorter mortgage, the lender usually will give you a lower interest rate.

## First-Time Home Buyer Programs

A recent trend in many communities across the nation is "first-time" home buyer educational programs. When you develop an interest in home ownership, you can sign up for one of these. There is little or no cost involved in enrolling in these programs. They are often sponsored by non-profit community services, sometimes with the government's help. In fact, Consumer Credit Counseling Services and many others conduct first-time home buyer seminars. In these programs, you get professional advice and valuable information about every aspect of how to choose and finance a home you can afford. In many cases, "graduates" receive financing incentives.

*ARMs — Adjustable Rate Mortgages*

For many decades, nearly all loans to purchase homes were made with an interest rate that stayed the same for the entire life of the mortgage — 30 years or otherwise. This is no longer the case. We have seen some rather wide swings in interest rates in the last two decades. When interest rates increased, the lenders had to pay more for the money they had loaned out on fixed-rate mortgages. Lenders have been caught with millions of dollars in outstanding loans made when rates were low. When rates rose, many lenders quickly found themselves in trouble. They were selling a product below cost — and that won't work very long. So, in the early 1980s, adjustable-rate mortgages became an alternative to the fixed-rate loan. Today, a large proportion of home loans are made on an adjustable-rate mortgage basis. Adjustable-rate mortgages are called ARMs.

An ARM is a mortgage which has a variable rate that "floats" with some specified index, such as prime rate. When that index changes, the interest rate on the ARM, subject to limitations, will also change. So, if the interest on an ARM changes, the payment that the homeowner makes each month also changes.

There are limitations to how much the ARM may change. In a mortgage contract, there may be provisions that limit how much the interest (and therefore the monthly payments) may go up or down. As only an exaggerated example, if interest rates double in one year during the life of an ARM, the rate the homeowner pays could not double.

Is an ARM a good bet for someone wishing to purchase a home? The answer depends. An ARM protects the lender from being hurt if the rate the lender has to pay for money rises. So, in return for this protection, the borrower is offered inducements to choose this type of mortgage. These inducements usually are in the form of a cheaper rate guaranteed for the first year or so of the mortgage. If interest rate swings during the mortgage are not too wild, both lender and borrower benefit from the ARM. If rates go down, the borrower benefits while the lender still makes money. However, if rates rise, the cost to the borrower (subject to the limits agreed upon in the mortgage) *will rise.* In other words, with an ARM the borrower takes the risk if interest rates rise during the life of the mortgage.

If a borrower wants a fixed-rate loan, and some do, a lender must factor their increased exposure to interest rate swings into the rate offered the borrower. Plain and simple, you don't get something for nothing. The borrower who wants the protection of a fixed-rate loan will pay a premium for that protection.

ARMs are very prevalent in today's market. Also, other types of consumer credit are often granted on an adjustable rate basis. Many credit cards have variable rates today. Even auto loans can have variable rates now. You need to know about these things.

### Financing an Automobile

This example may be of more interest to you because you probably will buy a car before you buy a house. The fact that you can save money when you borrow for a shorter term applies to a car loan as well as to a home loan. There are two additional and very important reasons people should go for the shorter loan when buying a car.

The first reason is that a car depreciates. This simply means it starts rapidly losing value the moment you drive it off the lot. If you finance it for too long, the car will be worth less than

*Financing a Car Is a Big Step*

what you owe on it for about the first three years. This is a potentially dangerous condition. The second reason is that many people don't want to drive the same car for very long. Styles change, cars get better, and many of us just don't want to drive the same car year after year.

In this first example, we keep things simple. There is no trade-in to worry about in these calculations. We're assuming that you have done a good job of bargaining and have gotten a good discount off the "sticker" price. Sales taxes, license and title, and the down payment are typical figures. We also assume you are being smart and have arranged your own insurance on the car.

| | |
|---|---:|
| Negotiated sales price...................... | $13,000 |
| State sales tax (7%)......................... | 910 |
| License and title........................... | 90 |
| Less your down payment.................... | (2,000) |
| Amount to finance.......................... | $12,000 |

Options for financing the $12,000 at 11 percent simple interest:

| Term | Monthly Payment | Total Payback | Increase |
|------|-----------------|---------------|----------|
| 36 payments..... | $392.87 ..... | $14,143.32 ..... | -0- |
| 48 payments..... | $310.15 ..... | $14,887.20 ..... | +$743.88 |
| 60 payments..... | $260.91 ..... | $15.654.60 ..... | +$1,511.28 |

While the monthly payments for the shorter periods are higher, look at how much you save. Financing for five years instead of three adds another 13 percent to the cost of the car. It also obligates your future income a lot longer.

There are, however, some other considerations of long-term financing. These things may cost you much more in practical terms than extra interest. Consider the following important points.

- If you financed this car for 36 months, in 18 months you would have it halfway paid for. The balance at that time would be $6,491.

  If you financed for 60 months, after 18 payments you still owe $9,061, or about two-thirds of the original amount borrowed.

- If you financed for 36 months and took good care of the car, after 18 payments you would have some "equity." That means that the car would be worth more than you owed. If you wanted a nicer car or were just plain tired of driving that one, you could use that equity to "trade up."

  If you had financed for 60 months, after 18 payments the car probably would be worth less than the balance owed. You would have "negative" equity. You probably would be married to the car for a very long time, whether you liked it or not.

So you see, while the smaller monthly payments can be attractive, they also can be a dangerous trap. Often it is better to bite the bullet and go for the larger payments.

### Leasing an Automobile

These days, many people do not buy a car; rather, they lease one. In fact, more than three out of ten car or truck deals involve a lease instead of a purchase. So, you need to know something about leasing.

*Because Automobile Leases Are Very Complicated, You Must Be Very Careful When Entering Into a Lease Transaction*

Although leasing may provide advantages for some people, an auto lease is, unfortunately, much more complicated than a straight purchase. People who do not completely understand a lease transaction are very likely to be taken advantage of by the companies that lease cars. A lease contract is typically more than three pages long, and it can be filled with a lot of legal terms in fine print. Some of the largest leasing companies are attempting to present the information in a lease agreement more clearly. Nevertheless, you have to be very careful when entering into a lease transaction. Be sure that you understand all of the terms to which you are agreeing.

Basically, when you lease a car or truck, you are simply paying for the *use* of that vehicle for a certain period of time and/or for a certain number of miles. When the term of the lease is over, the car goes back to the leasing company unless you decide to buy it or to lease it again. Because lease agreements are complex, it is often difficult to compare one with another. When you buy a car, it is fairly easy to compare the price from one dealer to another dealer, although financing alternatives can complicate that a bit. Leasing is a different matter.

The big advantage of leasing over purchasing a car is that the monthly payment is lower for the lease. That lower payment lures many people to lease an automobile rather than to buy one.

The big disadvantage is that you are only paying for the *use* of a car for a limited period of time, such as two or three years. After making monthly payments for all of that time, you have nothing to show for it. But you had use of the car—that's what you paid for.

Many lease contracts also put a limit on the number of miles that you can drive during the lease term. If you drive more miles than allowed, you have to pay a fee per mile. Lease agreements may include an expected value of the car at the end of the lease period. If the value of the car turns out to be less than that amount, you may have to pay the difference. On the other hand, if the value of the car is more than the stated amount, you could get the benefit of that difference. Of course, no one knows for sure today what a car will be worth, say, two or three years from now.

When leasing an automobile, do not focus only on the monthly payment. You have to first consider the vehicle's real selling price. That selling price should not be the list price, but rather a lower negotiated price. When you buy a car, you rarely pay the sticker price that appears on the window of a new car. Rather, you bargain with the dealer to get that price down. In the case of a lease, the lease payment should not be based on the sticker price, but rather on a price which you have negotiated down from the sticker price. That price of the vehicle is called the "capitalized cost." That capitalized cost also may include the license and registration fees.

On some lease deals, you have to make a down payment. That down payment may be in the form of a cash payment or the trade-in of an older vehicle. Any down payment should be subtracted from the capitalized cost. The difference is your "net capitalized cost."

If the dealer guarantees the value of the car at the end of the term of the lease, you would subtract that value from the net capitalized cost. That difference is the amount you are actually financing. It represents the loss of value (depreciation) over the life of the lease.

In addition to paying for the depreciation expected in the value of the vehicle, you also have to pay the leasing company for use of its money during the term of the lease. That payment is called the "lease charge." It is similar to the interest charge on a loan. In addition to the effective interest, some leasing companies will add other fees or expenses to the lease charge.

When you add the lease charge to the amount of the depreciation of the vehicle, you have the total payment. To find out how much you would pay each month, you simply divide that total payment by the number of months of the lease agreement.

To get the best deal in a lease, find out what the capitalized cost of the vehicle is, and try to get the leasing company to tell you about the lease charge. Negotiate with the leasing company on both items.

However, you cannot just compare the monthly payment amounts to determine the best deal. Other parts of the agreement may vary, as well. For example, the term of the lease may be different, the residual value may be different, the mileage limitation may be different, and other terms may vary from one lease to another.

***When Leasing an Automobile, It Is Very Important to Focus on the Net Capitalized Cost of the Vehicle***

It is very important to focus on the net capitalized cost of the vehicle. If you do not know that, you could end up paying much more than necessary over the term of the lease. Because so many people do not know all they should about leasing, they get the short end of the stick when they lease a vehicle. As with just about everything else in life, the more you know, the better off you are.

### Credit Cards — That Fantastic Plastic

What we take for granted today! A person who has established good credit can, armed with a little piece of plastic, go almost anywhere in the world and use his or her credit. You can get a cash advance on your credit card at almost any ATM, charge a meal, a room, or even a major purchase. Not too many years ago, before powerful computers, these things simply were not possible.

We think Western Union was the first company, in about 1914, to come up with a credit card. It was made of metal. The card was given to special customers allowing them interest-free deferred payments on their business with Western Union. In the 1930s, AT&T introduced a credit card for its customers. But not much else happened in the development of credit cards for a long time.

In the 1960s, BankAmericard and Master Charge came into being. Before long, these organizations went global, making these cards useable world wide. In 1977, BankAmericard changed its name to Visa, to make the name acceptable throughout other countries. Master Charge became MasterCard. The world was never to be the same again.

Both Visa and MasterCard are essentially licensing organizations. They do not issue cards or make the terms. They license banks, credit unions, S&Ls, and other financial institutions to use the name and the networking systems. Each institution is free to set its own terms on the use of the card.

More recently, several other large companies have entered the national and global market, offering their own cards. Some of these are rapidly gaining acceptance as universal credit cards also. Discover is an example of this. A Discover Card is not a MasterCard or Visa, but offers essentially the same product to consumers.

Today, non-financial firms offer Visa and MasterCard by arrangement with a lender. Examples are Exxon and General Motors, which enable you to earn discounts on their products as you use their credit cards.

When we talk about credit cards, we just may be talking about the most popular and most valued consumer product, or convenience, ever created. We are talking about big business! To give you some idea of what is going on in the world of credit cards, in 1994 consumers charged almost $300 *billion* on Visa cards alone! In that year there were over 200 million Visa cards in circulation just in the United States. And we're talking about a world-wide product. Remember also that these numbers we just gave you do not include MasterCard, Discover Card, American Express, or any of the thousands of retail cards being used, such as Sears, Montgomery Wards, or J. C. Penny.

If you were to lay end-to-end the 200 million Visa cards in circulation just in the U.S. at the present time, they would stretch almost 11,000 miles! That's the distance from New York to Egypt—and back!

Now, with any of the several cards offered, you can shop or travel almost anywhere, get cash out of your bank account from thousands of locations, and much more. You get one monthly bill, detailing all of your charges. You can pay the bill in full, often without any interest, or make smaller payments over a period of time (with interest). That can be a trap or a tool, depending on your discipline and management ability.

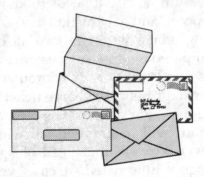

### Getting a Credit Card

One of the most intense and competitive marketing campaigns in our history has been going on for the last several years. All across America mailboxes are full of credit card solicitations. Many credit card companies are focusing their selling efforts on young adults, particularly college students. So, when you are ready to apply for your first credit card, you will not have to look very hard to find a credit card application.

To get a piece of the fantastic plastic, you apply to the card company of your choice. The company checks your credit and determines your capacity. Then it gives you a credit limit and issues you the card. Each card company has its specific terms, governed in certain ways by federal law (we talk about terms a little later). So long as you do not exceed your charge limit, do not abuse the privilege of using credit, and live up to the payment terms, you can enjoy the wonderful world of plastic.

Here is what happens when you use the card. This varies somewhat according to where you use the card. Because even more changes in automation are taking place, not every merchant has the same tools yet.

In a fully automated environment, the clerk rings up your sale, takes your card, and zips it through a small machine. Then, electronics take over. In just a few seconds, the machine reads the magnetic stripe on your card, calls another machine somewhere else in the world, and tells that machine about your purchase and everything else it needs to know to check your account. At this point, and in a fraction of a second, computers check your paying habits, the expiration date of your card, and the charge is compared against your balance and credit limit. In another few seconds, the clerk's computerized register receives the approval, prints your charge ticket which you sign, and the deal is done. Your account has been charged and the merchant's account will be credited, all with tiny electrical impulses sent over wires at the speed of light. Because the process is so highly automated, it costs very little and is incredibly fast.

If you are in Paris, France, and use your American Express Card, the approval involves a 46,000 mile electronic journey over telephone lines and computers!

The same card can be popped into an ATM. You can inquire about your account or get cash to go out on the town. To use an ATM, you need a PIN, or Personal Identification Number. That number comes from the issuer of your card. Never write down your PIN number. You don't want a thief to get your number and steal your money. When you insert your card in an ATM, the machine will ask you for your PIN. That number is matched up with your card. If correct, the machine will allow you to get money out of your account or check your balance.

Like any form of credit, the plastic kind can be a powerful tool. But for many people, credit cards can be a little harder to manage wisely. The cards require a higher degree of self-discipline. After all, they can be like carrying around a large supply of cash—cash you may not have. Many good and honest people who can manage other forms of credit get into trouble with credit cards. The cards are so easy to use. Most people quickly learn their lesson, get back on course, and are the wiser. But a few should avoid credit cards entirely. They just cannot resist the impulse buying that credit cards can make possible. Remember this when you get your first card.

If you apply for and receive a credit card, do not allow yourself to be a victim of fraud. Keep your credit card number private. Do not leave your statements, or anything with your account number on it, laying around. Never give your credit card number, or any other number such as your checking account number, to someone who calls you on the phone. Even if they have a good-sounding story about why they need your number, it may be a scam. You will wind up with charges on yor next statement that you know nothing about.

Remember also, not all cards are the same. Each can have different interest rates and other terms. Some states severely limit interest rates card companies can charge. Others permit much higher rates. We have seen rates vary from 9.9 to 23.99 percent on the unpaid balance. In addition, there can be heavy charges if the account balance goes over the authorized credit limit. Usually, there will also be extra charges for late payments. Many card agreements provide for no interest if the balance is paid in full each month. This is called a "grace period." You should check for this feature when shopping for a credit card.

In all cases, federal law requires each company to give you a written statement of all the terms of its cards. Many people don't take the time to check out this information. We hope you will not be one of these.

You might think we would be better off if the government required that interest rates be very low. This is not true. If rates were so low that these companies could not make a profit, this fantastic plastic would not be available for us.

### The "Secured Card"

Up until now, we have led you to believe you must have excellent credit to get a credit card. That is true, but in recent years there has been a product marketed for people who cannot qualify for a true credit card. This is called a "secured card." We mentioned the secured card in Chapter 7. A secured card is similar to a true credit card, but it must be secured by an actual savings deposit. You open a savings account with, say $400, and you get a secured card with, typically, a $400 limit. You are paid interest on the savings, but of course you pay a much higher rate of interest for the use of the card.

About the only good thing about these cards is that it is possible for people to establish credit with them, and later get a true credit card.

Remember that credit cards are but one form of consumer credit. They may be the most modern, they may be the most talked about, and they may appear to be very desirable. Properly used, with budgeting and discipline, they are all of these things and more. But for many people, credit cards are the most difficult form of credit to manage. That is because credit cards are so very convenient to use. Credit cards are not for everyone. Some people are better off using installment credit to obtain the better things in life (that they can afford). Installment credit has certain checks and balances against overuse. You must think about what you want to use installment credit for and why, and then arrange a loan for a specific amount of money for a specific length of time. It is much more difficult to make bad mistakes in judgment using installment credit than it is using a credit card.

## THINGS TO REMEMBER

Interest is the price you pay for the use of someone else's money.

The amount of interest you pay is determined by (1) the interest rate, (2) the amount of money involved, and (3) how long you use the money.

The only way a lender or retailer can make credit available is to charge interest.

Almost any contract will provide for late charges if the terms of the agreement are not kept. The *Disclosure Statement* will advise you of all costs or fees.

The "term" of a loan governs how fast you pay the money back. Paying back credit rapidly not only saves you interest, but regains your credit capacity that much quicker.

Collateral is property — anything of value — that the borrower pledges to the lender to reduce the lender's risk.

A person who has built a good credit record and has good income often can borrow without collateral.

The *Credit Application* is what gives the lender most of the information required. If that information meets a lender's basic credit policies, a credit report may be ordered from one or more credit bureaus to determine if that person has a history of satisfactory repayment.

The use of credit cards requires a high degree of management and discipline. Installment credit, or personal loans, are a more manageable form of credit for some people.

Protect your credit card numbers. Never give anyone who calls you your credit card number. You may wind up a victim of fraud.

# Chapter Ten

# All About Credit Bureaus

After Chuck filled in his credit application to finance his car, the lender saw that Chuck might be a good candidate for a loan. Of course, the lender needed more information about Chuck and his credit history. The lender knew that Chuck was young and would not have a long credit history, but it was necessary to check that Chuck did not have a bad record. So, the lender contacted a credit bureau.

When you have finished this chapter, you will fully understand the important role credit bureaus *will* play in your life. You will understand how they compile information about you. You will see how they make that information available to creditors you wish to do business with. You will learn how they help responsible consumers get credit by maintaining records of their good paying habits. You also will learn how credit bureaus help businesses who extend credit avoid making mistakes by *not* advancing credit to people who don't have a good record of paying debts.

Consider these facts:

- There are over 180 *million* active credit files in the U.S. today.

- Every year credit bureaus in the U.S. issue about 550 *million* credit reports.

- Americans with good credit enjoy the privilege of using more than $855 *billion* in consumer installment credit each year. This doesn't include credit to purchase homes!

There are three major credit reporting companies in the U.S. — Equifax Credit Information Services, Trans Union Corporation, and TRW Information Systems. Each of these companies owns many individual credit bureaus and each makes its files available to other, independently-owned credit bureaus. All of the big three, and most other credit bureaus, are members of Associated Credit Bureaus, Inc., an international trade association. These members follow a stringent Code of Ethics. These ethics are carefully designed to benefit and protect the public.

### What Is a Credit Bureau?

A credit bureau is a "credit reporting agency." That is the legal definition. Actually, a credit bureau is simply a company that gathers information on people who use credit. Credit bureaus sell that information to companies that grant credit. That information is called a "credit report." A credit bureau also may furnish a report to an employer to whom you apply for a job, or even to a prospective landlord whose apartment you want to rent. It will also supply information to many other legitimate kinds of inquirers who want to do business with you.

### Where Does a Credit Bureau Get Its Information About Me?

The information in a credit report is gathered from a number of sources. The information is usually referred to as "data." Most of the data come from creditors with whom you do business. Other data come from public records. If someone sues you — files a lawsuit claiming you owe him or her money — that information is public record. If you file for bankruptcy, that also is public record. It is on file at a courthouse for the world to see. Credit bureaus also pass data to other credit bureaus. If you move, your credit record follows you. You can run, but you can't hide!

P.O. Box 345
Any Town. USA

John Allan Doe
342 Oak Alley
Main Town, AL

Date: 11/15/95
Social Security Number 022-28-1852
Date of Birth 01/01/74

## CREDIT HISTORY

| Company Name | Account Number | Whose Acct. | Date Opened | Months Reviewed | Date Of Last Activity | High Credit | Terms | All Items as of Date Reported Balance | Past Due | Status | Date Reported |
|---|---|---|---|---|---|---|---|---|---|---|---|
| Any Bank | 123456 | I | 05/95 | 05 | 10/95 | 1205 | 55 | 930 | 0 | I1 | 10/95 |
| Good Jewelry | 2345678 | I | 06/94 | 12 | 09/95 | 375 | 35 | 35 | 0 | R1 | 10/95 |
| Home Furniture Company | 33333 | J | 03/95 | | 10/95 | 400 | 40 | 120 | 0 | I1 | 10/95 |
| Town Department Store | 1234-456-33333 | I | 08/94 | 10 | 06/95 | 300 | 25 | 0 | 0 | R1 | 08/95 |
| Bankcard | 4567-4332568953-33 | J | 07/95 | | 10/95 | 1000 | 20 | 100 | 0 | R1 | 10/95 |

Amount in H/C Column is Credit Limit

******************************Additional Information******************************************

>>>>>Former/Other Address  Box 536, Any Town

>>>>>Last Reported Employment  Management Trainee, XYZ Corp.

>>>>>Former/Other Employment  Part-Time, Stoney Point Pizza

************Companies That Requested Your Credit History***********************

| | | |
|---|---|---|
| 05/14/95 | Any Bank | 06/02/94 | Good Jewelry |
| 03/22/95 | Home Furniture Company | 08/13/94 | Town Department Store |
| 07/01/95 | Bankcard | | |

## EXPLANATION OF CODED INFORMATION

TYPE OF ACCOUNT:
Open account (30 days or 90 days) .............. O
Revolving or Option (open-end account) ........... R
Installment (fixed number of payments) ............. I

| CURRENT MANNER OF PAYMENT (Using Payments Past Due or Age from Due Date) | TYPE OF ACCOUNT | | |
|---|---|---|---|
| | O | R | I |
| Too new to rate; approved but not used | 0 | 0 | 0 |
| Pays (or paid) within 30 days of payment due date, or not over one payment past due | 1 | 1 | 1 |
| Pays (or paid) in more than 30 days from the payment due date, but not more than 60 days, or not more than two payments past due | 2 | 2 | 2 |
| Pays (or paid) in more than 60 days from payment due date, but not more than 90 days, or three payments past due | 3 | 3 | 3 |
| Pays (or paid) in more than 90 days from payment due date, but not more than 120 days, or four payments past due | 4 | 4 | 4 |
| Pays (or paid) in more than 120 days or more than four payments past due | 5 | 5 | 5 |
| Making regular payments under debtor's plan or similar arrangement | 7 | 7 | 7 |
| Repossession. (Indicate if it is voluntary return of merchandise by the consumer) | 8 | 8 | 8 |
| Bad debt | 9 | 9 | 9 |

◆ Sample Credit Report ◆

Credit Bureau of XXXXX
P.O. Box 123
Any Town, USA

Date: 11/15/95
Social Security Number 078-05-1120
Date of Birth 01/01/71

John Q. Fox
1677 Main Street
Any Town, USA

## CREDIT HISTORY

| Company Name | Account Number | Whose Acct. | Date Opened | Months Reviewed | Date Of Last Activity | High Credit | Terms | Balance | Past Due | Status | Date Reported |
|---|---|---|---|---|---|---|---|---|---|---|---|
| XYZ Bank | 987654 | I | 05/91 | | 01/93 | 2000 | 75 | 1400 | 1400 | I9 | 05/94 |
| | Charged Off Account | | | | | | | | | | |
| Good Jewelry | 5693678 | I | 04/91 | 12 | 06/93 | 600 | 50 | 550 | 550 | R9 | 10/95 |
| | Charged Off Account | | | | | | | | | | |
| Sam's Furniture | 23890 | I | 03/92 | | 02/93 | 900 | 45 | 675 | 675 | I9 | 10/95 |
| Corner Department Store | 2386-555-55893 | I | 08/91 | 10 | 06/93 | 300 | 25 | 250 | 250 | R9 | 08/95 |
| | Charged Off Account | | | | | | | | | | |
| Bankcard | 4599-46987-5681-21 | I | 07/92 | | 09/93 | 2000 | 40 | 1675 | 1675 | R9 | 10/95 |
| | Charged Off Account | | | | | | | | | | |

Amount in H/C Column is Credit Limit

*************************************Courthouse Records*******************************************
>>>>>Bankruptcy Filed 08/93  Case Number 345723
>>>>>Judgement Filed 06/93  City Court Case Number 456733  Defendant John Doe, Amount $300
>>>>>Lien Filed 12/94  Amount $4250, Class Federal
*************************************Additional Information***************************************
>>>>>Former/Other Address  1256 Morning Street, Kansas City Kansas
>>>>>Former/Other Address  Rt 2 Box 345, Dallas Texas
>>>>>Former/Other Address  12346 Willow Street, Baltimore MD
>>>>>Last Reported Employment  Laborer, Bullet Construction Company
>>>>>Other Employment  Carpenter Helper, Wild's Building Company
>>>>>Other Employment  Routsabout, Baytown Marine
*************************************Companies That Requested Your Credit History***************************

| | | | |
|---|---|---|---|
| 06/15/94 | Any Bank | 06/02/94 | Cornerstone Furniture |
| 03/12/94 | Home Furniture Company | 07/01/94 | Corner Bank and Trust |
| 07/10/94 | Auto Finance Company | 07/11/94 | Jim's Auto Sales |
| 07/01/95 | Bankcard | | |

### EXPLANATION OF CODED INFORMATION

WHOSE ACCOUNT (ECOA)

The Equal Credit Opportunity Act designators explain who is responsible for the account and the type of participation you have with the account.

J — Joint
I — Individual
U — Undesignated
A — Authorized User
T — Terminated
M — Maker
C — Co-Maker

B — On Behalf of another person
S — Shared

## What Information Is in My Credit Report?

Study the two sample credit reports in this section. One is that of a 21 year-old, off to a good start using credit wisely and building credit ratings. The other person, also young, obviously has had problems. Which would you lend money to?

Credit reports contain a lot of information. First, there is identification and employment data. This includes your name and address, your employer, your Social Security number, and maybe even your birthday. Other information, such as how long you've lived in the same place and whether or not you are a job-hopper, is of value to a creditor. After all that dull stuff comes the meat. A lot of information is tracked on your credit history. When did you start doing business? Whom have you done business with? What was the date of your last payment? How much credit was extended to you? How much do you owe now? Do you keep your word and pay on time? These companies, and the creditors who pay for the information, are only interested in information about your financial stability. They don't care about your social life or how you wear your hair.

## Why Do We Have Credit Bureaus?

It's very simple. People need credit, and companies can't extend credit without good information about who is a deadbeat and who pays bills on time. A hundred years ago, people couldn't get credit as we know it today. Back then, a farmer could go to the local bank and make a loan to buy seed. He paid for it when the crop came in. But the guy at the bank knew the farmer, knew his reputation, and knew he wasn't going to run off anywhere. Big companies or large landowners could get credit because they had collateral. The rest of us who were not well known were out of luck. However, we didn't need credit then, because those cars and TVs were not available to buy! Now, credit makes the world go around. We need credit bureaus to collect and make available the information necessary to have credit transactions.

## How to Find Out About Your Credit Report

Your credit bureau record probably will get started the first time you apply for credit. There won't be much information on file at first. Your data will grow as you build a credit history. There are some very important things you need to know. Suppose you are denied credit because of information in a credit bureau file. The creditor is required by law to notify you of the name and address of the credit bureau that supplied any information to it. If you contact that credit bureau within 30 days to learn what is in your credit file, you are entitled to that information at no charge.

*You Can Obtain a Copy of Your Credit
Report at Any Time for a Small Fee*

You are entitled to learn what is in your file at any time. There will be a small charge, usually from $5 to $10. The yellow pages of the telephone book will tell you the name (or names) of the credit bureaus in your area. Call and find out the rules. Credit bureau representatives won't tell you about your report on the phone. When you properly identify yourself, they may mail you a copy or make an appointment for you to come in and see your report. Most cities have two and sometimes three credit bureaus. Several are very large national companies with hundreds of offices. That competition makes credit bureaus work harder to collect more and accurate data. Competition also keeps prices down by avoiding a monopoly.

## What if My Credit Report Is Wrong?

Most credit reports are very accurate. This is the result of competition. If a credit bureau gets a reputation for producing wrong information, creditors won't pay for that bureau's reports. It will go out of business. However, errors can happen.

We recommend that people check their report every two to four years. If you find any wrong information in your file, the law gives you the right to get it corrected without charge. If you discover incorrect information, the credit bureau must recheck the source and correct the information if it is wrong. If the information is on somebody else, the credit bureau must remove it. If the information cannot be verified, the credit bureau also must remove it.

There can be what is called an omission. This is when you may have some good credit that simply isn't in your file. The law does not require a credit bureau to have everything. But for a small fee most credit bureaus will "update" your report. The credit bureau will check your references and include that data in your report.

## What if I Have Derogatory Information in My Report?

If that information is accurate, tough luck! You get what you earn. If you have earned a good credit file by paying your bills on time, you enjoy the rewards. If you have been irresponsible, you pay the price for that by having a bad credit report.

There is a provision designed to help anyone who incurs a derogatory rating due to an offsetting circumstance. The Fair Credit Reporting Act provides that a consumer may place a message of 100 words or less in his or her credit report. This can be very helpful if there is a dispute about a debt. It may also be helpful if there were temporary problems, such as unemployment, that caused a poor rating in an otherwise good report.

Negative information, often referred to as "derogatory," that is correct cannot be removed from your file. There is nothing you or anyone else can do to force a credit bureau to remove information that is accurate. So-called "credit doctors" or "credit repair services" may claim to be able to remove bad information from your file. Only a dummy believes that he or she can get good credit when it is not deserved.

Derogatory information can include judgments, liens, accounts turned over to collection agencies, charge-offs, late payments, and repossessions. It also includes, of course, that financial failure called bankruptcy.

Most of the time, bad credit ratings are well deserved. Sometimes, however, people can get into trouble through problems they can't help. Loss of income and poor health are just two of the uncertainties we all face in life. If individuals haven't used too much credit and if they have some savings, they should be able to weather a little storm without it raining on their credit.

When good, honest folks get into credit trouble, there's hope. If the problem is too much debt, non-profit counseling agencies such as Consumer Credit Counseling Services usually can help by getting creditors to cooperate with a common-sense repayment plan. Even if the problem is simply self-discipline or personal management, these agencies can often help through counseling. If a person faces problems squarely, gets on a strict budget, and avoids using credit for a while, the debts get paid. That person's credit report will begin to improve again.

### How Long Can Derogatory Information Remain on File?

The Fair Credit Reporting Act also governs how long bad credit stays on a report. Most of it stays for seven years. But there are important exceptions. Bankruptcy can stay on for 10 years! And there are three circumstances where a bankruptcy can be reported forever. They are when someone applies for credit in an amount larger than $50,000; for a life insurance policy of $50,000 or more; or for an application for a job that pays $20,000 or more and the employer gets a credit report in connection with the job application.

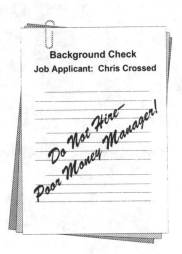

Bad credit can affect your chances of getting a job. Many employers get credit reports on applicants. Would you want somebody who doesn't pay his or her bills working for you?

**Credit Repair Clinics**

In recent years, somebody figured out a new way to make money from ignorant or lazy people. Credit repair companies claim they can "fix" or "clean up" or "repair" bad credit. We've already told you that nobody can make a credit bureau remove bad ratings if they are correct! The Fair Credit Reporting Act gives *you* the right to have any incorrect information corrected or removed *FREE!* The Federal Trade Commission has recently issued warnings to the public about "credit repair" companies and some of the things they claim to do. Only an ignorant or lazy person is going to pay one of these companies hundreds of dollars and more to do it for him or her. Remember, a fool and his money are soon parted.

# THINGS TO REMEMBER

A credit bureau is a company that gathers information on people who use credit. A credit bureau then sells this information to creditors needing the data to make good credit decisions. This information can also be supplied to others for legitimate purposes, such as employment decisions or landlord-lessee decisions.

A credit bureau gathers information primarily from companies you do business with and from public records.

A credit report contains data such as whom you owe, how much you owe those creditors, and how you have paid your bills. It can contain other information such as employment.

The Fair Credit Reporting Act gives you the right to find out what is contained in your credit report. If you are turned down for credit, that same law requires the creditor to notify you of the credit bureau that supplied the information on which the decision was based.

If your credit report contains inaccurate information, there is a good, workable process whereby you may get the information corrected.

If a person has not paid his or her bills promptly, as agreed, there is no legal way to get bad ratings off the record. Bad ratings are the price of not paying accounts properly. Derogatory information, such as paying slowly, can stay on a record for seven years. A bankruptcy filing can remain for 10 years.

There are non-profit Consumer Credit Counseling Services all across the country. They usually can help the honest person in trouble get back on his or her feet and on the way to a good financial future.

Never sign anything or pay a fee to anyone who tells you he or she can get bad ratings removed from your credit report. If negative information is accurate, you are stuck with it.

# Chapter Eleven

# Making A Checking Account Work For You

When Chuck Taylor got his first part-time job several years ago, he opened a checking account at a nearby bank. Having the account was convenient for him, and he knew the bank was a safe place to keep his money. Also, Chuck found that he made good contacts at the bank — people who had an interest in him later when he wanted that car loan.

As Chuck discovered, there is a lot to know about checking accounts. And it's all important because a checking account, properly used, is a building block of good money management.

**All About Checking Accounts**

Everybody knows what a checking account is and how it is used. Can you imagine life without this simple but powerful tool? Imagine your parents or your teacher carrying around all of their cash. Imagine them driving to the bank to get money out of an account every time they went to the store. Imagine business people carrying around suitcases full of cash to close a deal. All business activity would grind to a slow crawl.

Today you can get a checking account at a commercial bank, a credit union, or a savings and loan association. You can write checks against accounts at some money market mutual funds, too.

Unless you keep a large amount of money in a checking account, you will pay service charges that reflect the cost of providing you the service. These service charges can vary widely from institution to institution. On top of that, most institutions offer several different types of accounts so that you can choose the one that best fits your needs. You must learn how to shop for services. You need to recognize those services that are best for you.

*Choosing an Account*

It is easy to choose the kind of account you want. And it is easy to pick a bank, credit union, or savings and loan. If members of your family do business at the Corner Bank and are happy with the service there, that bank would be a good choice for you. Just stop by the office and tell someone that you wish to open a checking account. If you are neat and your hair isn't three colors, you should get a nice welcome. When you sit down with an officer, ask him or her to explain the options. There are many kinds of checking accounts.

*The Kinds of Accounts*

We can't tell you about all the different accounts you will be offered in a rapidly changing market. But there will probably be an account that will be free if you keep a minimum balance of, say, $500.

If you are not able to maintain a high balance, there may be an account with a very small monthly charge, typically two or three dollars a month. Usually with this account, you have to limit your check writing to a certain number of checks (maybe 20) a month. With this account, you would not be required to keep a minimum balance.

Let's hope you don't turn out to be one of those people who write checks at the local convenience store for two dollars! It is a source of amazement to us (and profit to the people who print checks) as to why some people insist on writing ridiculous numbers of small checks every month. Cash does have its place.

Some accounts may limit the number of free teller or ATM (Automated Teller Machine) transactions you can have each month. After that number, the bank will charge you. The charge may range from a quarter to a dollar or more for each transaction.

There are many institutions that offer free accounts to students in high school and college. You should definitely check out this possibility if you qualify.

### Other Costs and Charges

Chuck learned that almost all accounts involve a charge for printed checks. Most banks have plain, low-cost checks and also very expensive, fancy checks. It may make you feel good to write checks printed with beautiful scenes. But you are going to pay extra for those checks. That's your choice to make. You should also ask if it costs extra to have your driver's license number, phone number, and other information printed on the checks. You may not want all this information on your checks. However, most merchants are going to ask you for it anyway when you use your checks.

## NSF (Non-Sufficient Funds) Checks

You are going to be charged if you write checks without having enough money in your account to cover them. That charge will probably be $15 or more. You must not misuse your account and let this happen to you. You see, writing an NSF check can cost you a lot more than the institution's charge. It can become a source of serious trouble.

A bank has two choices when you write an NSF check. It can return (bounce) the check, or it can pay the check as a courtesy to you. Many institutions will pay the check if the shortage is not too large. This is called an overdraft. Either way, you will pay a charge. Your bank will be more likely to pay (overdraft) an accidental NSF check if you do not have a history of writing NSF checks. The institution is not under any obligation to pay a bad check, not even for one penny! You are not supposed to write an NSF check, period. Under certain circumstances, if you write a bad check, you may violate a criminal law.

Whether the institution pays or bounces the check, you will be sent a notice advising you of the action. The notice will tell you the amount of the charge (the institution's fee) for the bad check your wrote. You should enter that charge in your stubs, or check record, right then. Otherwise you may forget it and could cause yourself even more embarrassment and expense later.

If the bank returns the check to the merchant who deposited it, you have messed up the merchant's account with his or her bank. This is because that merchant's bank will charge the merchant's account for the worthless deposit. The merchant made a deposit expecting your check to be honored. If one of your checks should be returned, contact the merchant immediately.

If you know for a fact that you have straightened out the problem in your account, you may ask the merchant to redeposit the check. However, the merchant instead may require you to come by and make the check good in cash. You also may have to pay the merchant a fee up to $25 for having caused the trouble. If this is the case, do so immediately. Don't forget—the merchant took your check fully expecting it to be good.

If you have written several bad checks, your problems are multiplied. In any case, find out what happened. If there was an error made in your account, straighten it out. If you cannot immediately understand what the problem is, call the institution. Ask for an appointment to see someone for help. Someone will sit down with you and help you figure out what has happened and how to straighten things out. Above all, remember that you must communicate. The worst thing you can do is to do nothing. Take the initiative to make things right.

## How to Avoid Messing up Your Checking Account

Chuck Taylor found out the hard way that you can mess up your account by failing to enter the amount in the stubs immediately after writing a check. He once found a check missing from his book. It wasn't really missing! It just was not entered in the stubs. He remembered writing the check but could not remember how much the check was for. He was a little embarrassed, but he called the store where he wrote it. The clerk was nice enough to look it up. The next time you write a check, see how long it takes to properly and completely record the transaction in your checkbook. It's probably not more that eight seconds. In Chuck's case, he learned a lesson without doing harm. Because he was not constantly drawing his bank account down to a low balance. he had enough money in the bank to cover his mistake.

*You Should Balance Your Checkbook Promptly to*
*Avoid Costly and Embarrassing Errors*

Also, you can mess up your account by not promptly balancing, or reconciling, your checkbook when the bank statement comes in. The reason it is so important to balance your checking account promptly each month is that you will, sooner or later, make simple errors during the month. Without prompt balancing, these errors will be undetected. Several small errors may pile up, or you may make one big error, and before you know it you have problems.

Balancing your checkbook really is easy and quick — once you learn how. And, learning how is easy also! Next, we explain a few basic, but important, terms you need to know. Then, we show you how easy it is to keep a checkbook straight.

## *Outstanding Check(s)*

This term simply means that one or more checks that you have written have not yet been paid against your account at your bank. Usually a check will clear promptly. However, it is not unusual for a check to take up to a week or more to reach your bank. If you handle your account right by entering and subtracting checks in your checkbook or check register when you write them, outstanding checks will never cause you a problem. The only time you even need to know anything about outstanding checks is when you reconcile (balance) your checkbook with your bank statement.

## *Reconciling Item*

This term refers to an item other than a check that must be taken into account when you balance your checkbook. It must be recorded and entered into your checkbook. The item usually will be a service charge, a charge for printed checks, interest the bank has paid you, or something similar.

## *Transit Item*

A transit item is a deposit that you have made but which has not yet been posted to your bank account. It is said to be "in transit." Remember something simple but important. If your deposit has not been posted to your account or if the money has not yet been collected by the bank (if the deposit was a check or a money order) your money is not there to be used. In other words, don't write checks before your deposit gets to the bank and has time to be credited! Your institution will tell you its rules. Some institutions "cut off" transactions at 2:00 p.m. All transactions after that time are posted the next day. If you deposit by mail, allow time for your deposit to be received and posted. When it comes time to reconcile your statement, you may have to consider a "deposit in transit."

### Availability of Funds

This term refers to a delay your bank may impose on your access to funds when you deposit checks drawn against another institution. For example, suppose for your birthday Grandma sends you a check drawn on Another State Bank and Trust located in Grandma's home town. After you deposit it, you should allow a few days for it to clear before you try to cash one of your own checks. After all, you can't expect your bank to pay out money before it gets the money from Grandma's bank! If you have a job that pays with an out-of-state check, it might be a good idea to ask your institution what the clearing time is. A federal law specifies how soon an institution must make your funds available. There is information on display at the bank or other institution giving you details.

### Overdraft

An overdraft is created when you write a check for which you do not have enough money, and the bank decides to honor your check. You are now "overdrawn." The bank has shown you a courtesy by honoring the check. The bank is not under any obligation to pay on your NSF check. Frankly, most banks will not even consider that unless you have a good record. If you write NSF checks too often, that good record will be lost. Even if the bank does honor your check, there will be a charge for the service. As in the case of any charge, you must enter it in your stubs or your account will be out of balance.

If you have a credit card with the bank, you can set up "overdraft privileges." This arrangement covers an NSF check by charging your credit card and putting the money in your checking account to clear the check. Usually, however, the minimum amount the bank will charge your credit card is $100. This is true even if you were only short a few dollars in your checking account. Of course, you pay a fee for this service. It may be a good idea to have this feature, just in case you make an honest mistake in your checking account. But, if you get sloppy with your account, or just use the feature too often, it can get expensive.

### Endorsements and Other Details

Any check you deposit must have been drawn (written) properly and endorsed (signed on the back) correctly. The numeric and written amounts must agree, and the signature must be correct. Also, you must endorse it on the back exactly as it was made out. In other words, if Chuck received a check made payable to C. W. Taylor, Chuck must sign it on the back "C. W. Taylor."

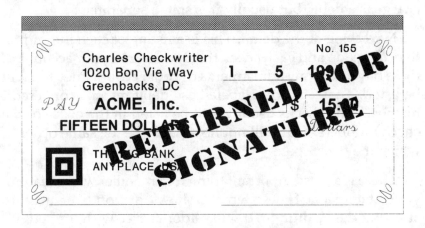

***Checks Must Be Filled Out Properly and Completely or They Will Be Returned***

There are a few other details you need to learn to avoid trouble. The most important is that you are fully responsible for any checks that you deposit into your account. In other words, if you deposit a check that bounces, the bank is going to charge your account for it. The check will be mailed back to you with an explanation. It's not the institution's job to collect it for you. Your gripe is with whoever gave you the check, not with the bank. Common sense and acceptance of responsibility will enable you to avoid most problems.

### Reading Your Bank Statement

Your bank statement is a monthly summary of activity that the institution has posted to your account. It is very important that you learn how to read your bank statement. It really isn't hard. Statements from different banks may not look alike, but they all show the same things.

First, look at the summary information. It starts with your beginning balance for the one-month period. It shows the total of deposits that the institution has received during the month (credits), the total of checks charged against your account for the month (debits), and finally, the ending balance. The service charge is a debit, but usually it is stated separately.

Next, look at the detail. This is a listing of each individual deposit made and each check that has cleared your account. If there have been any adjustments to your account, they too will be listed. They are often labeled as "debit memos" or "credit memos." The checks usually will be listed in the order of the check numbers. This will not necessarily be the same order in which they were paid.

There is a very important thing to remember when reading your statement. The statement shows a month of activity affecting the institution. It will seldom agree with the activity in your checkbook. This is because of the time it takes checks to clear your account. On occasion, there may be a deposit in transit. But don't worry about this now. It will all be very clear when you reconcile your checkbook with the bank statement. Never change your checkbook until you have reconciled it with the bank and positively identified any reason for change.

### Reconciling Your Checkbook

Reconciling your checkbook involves proving that your records agree with the bank statement. It consists of a few steps and simple math. Follow along, referring to the illustrations on pages 140–143, and you will see how easy it is. We assume you are starting with the first monthly statement on a new account or one that was in balance the prior month.

Your bank statement probably will have a fill-in-the-blanks form printed on the back to help you balance, as does the one in the illustration. We show you a little short cut. It is the same process, but will save you some time and writing.

### Step One — Identify the Paid Checks

This is simple. The real purpose is not so much to identify the paid checks as to pin down the "outstanding" ones. Somewhere in your checkbook stubs there will be a margin or an unused column where you can make a mark or an X. First, look at your bank statement to see which checks have been listed (paid). Next, make a small mark in your checkbook for each of your checks that have cleared the bank. Third, make a list of those checks that you have written but which are not listed on your statement. Include all of them right up to the last one you wrote. Add them up and jot down the total. If you are using the form on the back of the statement, there will be a place for listing these checks and the total. You have now identified your *Outstanding Checks*. Remember that term?

### Step Two — Deposits in Transit

You may not have any of these gems, but at least find out for sure. Look in your checkbook and see if all recent deposits that you have made are listed on your statement. If not, the total of these will be *Deposits in Transit*. Write this figure down or enter it on the form.

### Step Three — Reconciling Items

Now look for any "reconciling items." Your service charge, if any, will be one of these. There may be a charge for printed checks if you recently ordered some. The items just mentioned should be subtracted from the balance in your checkbook. If you were paid interest, add that positive reconciling item. If you are using the form, there is a place for this total. If not, just write down the total, making sure you have the value (positive

**ANY TOWN BANK**
P.O. BOX 9999
ANY TOWN, LA  70000
(800) 555-5555

JULY              23, 1995
ACCOUNT #10000000000000

MEMBER FDIC

MR. JOHN Q. DOE
1234 ANY STREET
ANY TOWN, LA  70000-0000

| BALANCE LAST STATEMENT | DEPOSITS & CREDITS | | CHECKS & WITHDRAWALS | | SERVICE CHARGE | BALANCE THIS STATEMENT |
|---|---|---|---|---|---|---|
| | NO. | TOTAL AMOUNT | NO. | TOTAL AMOUNT | | |
| 75.00 | 2 | 450.00 | 8 | 161.90 | 12.00 | 351.10 |

CLUB ACCOUNT                                    ACCOUNT NUMBER:  1000000000000

U.S. SAVINGS BONDS ARE TAX-FREE FOR EDUCATION.  IT'S SMARTER THAN EVER TO
START SAVING TODAY.

DEPOSITS AND NON-CHECK TRANSACTIONS

| | | | |
|---|---|---|---|
| 7/01 | 225.00 | Deposit | |
| 7/15 | 225.00 | Deposit | |
| 7/15 | 1.00 | Checksmart Fee | 1234567890123456789 |
| 7/15 | 3.00 | Bill Payer Service Chrg | 0000000012345 |
| 7/17 | 1.00 | Maintenance Fee | OD Protection |
| 7/23 | 12.00 | Service Charge | |

CHECKS

| DATE | CHECK NO | AMOUNT | DATE | CHECK NO | AMOUNT |
|---|---|---|---|---|---|
| 7/13 | 540 | 65.00 | 7/14 | 542 | 37.25 |
| 7/15 | 543 | 20.00 | 7/18 | 544 | 34.65 |

PAGE    1

THIS FORM IS PROVIDED TO HELP YOU
RECONCILE YOUR CHECKING ACCOUNT

CHECKS OUTSTANDING
(Those written which have
not cleared the bank)

| NO. | $ | |
|---|---|---|
| | | |
| | | |
| | | |
| | | |
| | | |
| | | |
| | | |
| | | |
| | | |
| | | |
| | | |
| | | |
| | | |
| | | |
| | | |
| | | |
| | | |
| TOTAL | $ | |

(1)  BANK BALANCE
     Shown on this
       statement          $ _____

(2)  ADD    (If Any)
     Deposits not shown
     on this statement    _____

(3)  TOTAL               $ _____

(4)  SUBTRACT
     Outstanding checks   _____

(5)  BALANCE (Should
     agree with your
     checkbook balance)   $ _____

This balance should agree with your
checkbook balance after deducting
charges (if any) and adding any interest
earned as shown on this statement.

If you have any questions or problems
related to this statement or any of your
bank accounts, please contact the branch
where you do business.  Your personal
banker will be pleased to be of assistance.

| NUMBER | DATE | TRANSACTION DESCRIPTION | PAYMENT (-) WITHDRAWAL | √T | FEE (-) IF ANY | AMOUNT OF DEPOSIT (+) | BALANCE |
|---|---|---|---|---|---|---|---|
| | | | | | | | 75.00 |
| | 7/1 | Deposit | | | | 225 00 | +225 00 |
| | | | | | | | 300 00 |
| 540 | 7/4 | J. C. Penney Homecoming Outfit | 65 00 | | | | -65 00 |
| | | | | | | | 235 00 |
| 541 | 7/10 | Allstate Insurance Car Insur. | 126 59 | | | | -126 59 |
| | | | | | | | 108 41 |
| 542 | 7/12 | Wal-Mart | 37 25 | | | | -37 25 |
| | | | | | | | 71 16 |
| | 7/15 | Deposit | | | | 225 00 | +225 00 |
| | | | | | | | 296 16 |
| 543 | 7/15 | Cash | 20 00 | | | | -20 00 |
| | | | | | | | 276 16 |
| 544 | 7/16 | Record Bar | 34 65 | | | | -34 65 |
| | | | | | | | 241 51 |

| NUMBER | DATE | TRANSACTION DESCRIPTION | PAYMENT (-) WITHDRAWAL | √ T | FEE (-) IF ANY | AMOUNT OF DEPOSIT (+) | BALANCE |
|---|---|---|---|---|---|---|---|
| 545 | 7/18 | Crocker Barrel Gas | 16 00 | | | | 241 51 |
| | | | | | | | -16 00 |
| | | | | | | | 225 51 |
| | 7/15 | Checksmart Fee | 1 00 | | | | -1 00 |
| | | | | | | | 224 51 |
| | 7/15 | Bill Payer Serv. Chrg. | 3 00 | | | | -3 00 |
| | | | | | | | 221 51 |
| | 7/17 | Maintenance Fee | 1 00 | | | | -1 00 |
| | | | | | | | 220 51 |
| | 7/23 | Service Charge | 12 00 | | | | -12 00 |
| | | | | | | | 208 51 |

BE SURE TO DEDUCT ANY PER ITEM CHARGES, SERVICE CHARGES, OR AUTOMATIC TELLER TRANSACTIONS. WHEN APPLICABLE, ADD INTEREST EARNED. BE SURE TO RECORD ALL PREAUTHORIZED PAYMENTS/DEPOSITS ON DATE SCHEDULED.

or negative) correct. Make sure you enter in your checkbook any charges against your account or interest that was paid to your account.

### *Step Four—Balancing Your Checkbook*

The first three steps were preparation. Now comes the simple math. Take the ENDING BALANCE, subtract your OUTSTANDING CHECKS, add any DEPOSITS IN TRANSIT, add and/or subtract any RECONCILING ITEMS (usually subtract), and the result should equal the balance shown in your checkbook. Now, wasn't that easy? Amazing! One, two, three, four!

**Don't Be Discouraged if You Don't
Balance on the First Try**

Okay, so something went wrong, and you're out of whack. Don't get discouraged or lose faith. This is exactly why you balance your checkbook to begin with. If you have made an error in your records, you want to know about it. This gives you a chance to find and correct it before you unknowingly write an NSF check.

Let's get started on finding that error. There are some logical things to look for. First, of course, recheck your math. Go back over your figures, and be careful not to make the same mistake twice. If that didn't do it, the next thing to do is to recheck the total of the outstanding checks you are subtracting from the ending statement balance (Step One). Next, bite the bullet and recheck all the math in your checkbook since the last time you proved your balance was right. This is a source of common mistakes that don't get corrected until you balance your checkbook each month.

If you still have not found the error, you need to start checking some detail. Take each paid check that came with the bank statement and compare it with the amount you entered in your book when you wrote each check. You could have transposed two digits, such as writing the check for $11.43 but entering it as $11.34.

If you are still messed up, look for what is called an "encoding error." This is a step that occurs at a bank. A real live human reads the amount of the check and causes a machine to print an "encoded" amount on the bottom right of the face of the check. The machine prints this encoded amount with magnetic ink. This way other machines can read the numbers. It doesn't happen often, but mistakes can be made in encoding checks.

If you find a mistake, call the institution. Give someone the information on the check. Your bank has a picture of it, and someone can see if a mistake was made. Someone will then enter a correction, or adjustment, on your account. That adjustment will show up on your next statement. Ask the banker to send you a memo so you don't have to wait for your next statement to be sure that the correction was made. Do not adjust your checkbook. The bank is telling you that a correction is being made. You should automatically be in balance next month without doing anything. Of course, all this assumes that the amount of the mistake agrees with the amount of the error you discovered. If so, all is okay. But it is not uncommon for there to be multiple errors (usually yours) in one statement. So keep looking until you find every mistake.

There are still one or two rare curve balls that might come your way. It is possible, but unlikely, that once or twice in your life someone else's check could get paid against your account. Also, your deposit could get posted to someone else's account. These occasions are rare, but they represent more reasons to reconcile your account each month.

Now you know all about handling your checking account. You now know a lot more than do people who go through life frequently messing up their accounts.

### ATM (Automated Teller Machine)

Another example of how technology is making our lives easier is the ATM. These machines are valuable and convenient tools. They are also cheaper for an institution to operate than a regular branch office. There is no other way a bank, credit union, or savings and loan could give you access to your money all night and all over the world.

These machines, and the use of them, have really caught on with consumers. To give you some idea of how popular they are, today there are over 125,000 of them in the United States alone. And, the number of ATMs has been growing at 15 percent per year.

But, ATMs must be treated with a great deal of respect, like any other powerful tool. Many people use an ATM because of the convenience. They can easily get cash from their checking account. But, a lot of people have messed up their checking account by using an ATM and failing to enter the transaction in their checkbook right then and later forgetting about it. Later, they get a notice that an NSF check has hit the bank, and they can't figure out why.

To use an ATM, you must first open a checking or savings account with a financial institution. You then are issued an ATM card, which is magnetically encoded with data so that the data can be read when the card is inserted into an ATM. When your account is opened, a computer randomly assigns you a PIN (Personal Identification Number). This is a secret number. You may rest assured that no one at the bank knows what it is.

When you insert your card into the ATM, the machine "reads" the magnetic stripe and knows who you are. The ATM video screen asks you for your PIN. If you correctly enter your PIN, you have access to your accounts. You may inquire about any account you have with the institution, withdraw money from your checking or savings account, or even transfer money from one account to another.

The convenience of ATMs does raise a security issue. Because banks care very much about your safety, many publish safety tips for their customers. Because this is so important, we have published common tips below.

- Treat your ATM card like cash, checks, and credit cards. Protect it. If it's lost or stolen, report it to the financial institution immediately.

- Memorize your PIN (personal identification number). Don't write it on your card or store it in your wallet. Don't give it out on the phone. Don't tell it to anyone — not even family, friends, or bank employees.

- Check out the area before using an ATM. If it is poorly lit, or if you see someone suspicious, use another ATM. Report any lighting or safety problem to the institution. If you suspect or witness unusual activity, contact the police immediately.

- Be courteous when waiting to use an ATM. Give the person using it the same privacy you expect.

- Try not to use an ATM alone at night.

- Minimize the time you spend at an ATM. Have your card ready. Have all forms filled out beforehand.

- Stand between the ATM and those waiting behind you in order to block their view of your transactions.

- If you feel uncomfortable during an ATM transaction, hit the CANCEL key to stop the transaction and get your card back. Leave the area immediately.

- As soon as you've completed your ATM transaction, take your card, money, and receipt, and move away from the teller machine. Put your cash in your wallet or purse right away. Don't count it or expose it so that others can see it.

- Don't forget to take your receipt. You'll need it to verify the transaction against your monthly account statement.

- If someone demands money from you at the ATM, do not resist. Carefully note the description of the person(s), and immediately call the police.

- If someone appears to be following you after you've left the ATM, drive to the nearest well-lit, well-populated area. Don't drive straight home.

- Stay alert while using the ATM. Be aware of your surroundings as you approach or leave the area. Stay visible while at the ATM and while moving to or from your car.

- Keep your engine running when using a drive-up ATM, so you can leave the area quickly.

If you are using a night depository, some of the same cautions will apply.

Charges for using an ATM can vary widely. You must find out about the fees your institution charges. If you use an ATM frequently, you can rack up big charges. Take responsibility, and make sure that you get the most for your money.

## Debit Cards

Debit cards have been much slower to catch on with consumers, but are now gaining popularity. Basically the debit card allows you to "write a check" without writing a check. Present your debit card when making a purchase and, assuming you have enough money in your checking account, the deal is done. The amount of purchase is immediately subtracted from your account balance and added to the merchant's bank account. It's all done electronically, and with the same machine used for credit card purchases. You don't have to worry about the hassles of writing a check and the merchant approving it.

When using a debit card, you must be sure to immediately enter the transaction in your checkbook, or register. Otherwise, you will forget.

## Banking by Phone

Many, if not most, banks today offer automated telephone service. You can telephone in 24 hours a day and perform all sorts of functions. With most institutions you can inquire about your current balance, get the details of your last transactions, find out how much interest you've earned, see if a check has cleared, transfer funds between accounts, issue a Stop Payment Request, reorder printed checks, and often many other functions. With most systems, when the bank is closed, you can even leave a message after hours for someone to call you back! In most cases, the institution allows a very generous number of these services free each month. By combining modern technology with telephones, these fast and user-friendly systems can save you a time.

## THINGS TO REMEMBER

A checking account is a powerful tool for managing money. It provides protection as well as convenience.

There are many kinds of checking accounts. When you open a checking account, learn about the choices and make the right one for you.

There is a time to use cash and a time to write checks. Don't be one of the people who flood the system with checks for just two or three dollars.

Writing a check without money in your account can lead to serious credit and legal problems. If you ever do make an honest mistake and write an NSF check, take care of it immediately.

A bank statement is a monthly summary of activity the bank has posted to your account. It may not always match the entries in your checkbook.

Balancing your checkbook each month with your bank statement will enable you to avoid unnecessary problems.

ATM machines offer a quick and convenient way to get money from your account and to conduct other banking business. But, as with any tool, you must learn to use ATMs properly.

A PIN must be kept secret.

Using a Debit Card is like writing a check electronically.

# Part Three

# The Basics of Insurance and Taxes

# Chapter Twelve

# Car Insurance

Chuck Taylor was on his way home from work one evening. It was just seven months after he bought his neat car. As he was passing through an intersection, some guy in a pickup truck ran a red light. There was a collision. Even though Chuck wasn't to blame, the right front fender and door of his car were smashed. Talk about a sick feeling! Chuck almost couldn't look at the damage. He was thankful, however, that he wasn't hurt in the accident.

Damage to Chuck's car amounted to over $2,100. He had used nearly all of his savings for the down payment when he bought his car. How would he pay the repair bill? Fortunately, both Chuck and the driver of the pickup had "full" coverage insurance. Chuck was well covered from the financial damage of the wreck.

Here is another story — it really happened. For most of a year, a granddaughter of one of the authors had been saving money for an automobile. She had been working part-time at J. C. Penny while in high school, depending upon parents and friends for transportation. Getting to and from school and work was a real problem. She had been a very responsible daughter and got her driver's license at age 16. Her parents agreed that she would be allowed to buy a car if she wanted it bad enough to save the money.

She saved rapidly because she was able to work a lot of hours and maintain her grades. She recently bought a real clean six-year old Toyota hatchback for $2,500. She had not quite saved the full amount of the purchase price plus sales tax. But it was an exceptional buy, so her parents loaned her the $500 necessary to complete the deal. Of course, the law, and her parents, required that she buy liability insurance at least.

She decided to purchase just liability insurance. Collision and comprehensive would have cost another $40 every six months; so, she chose not to purchase the "extra" coverage. After all, she wasn't planning to need it! On the 13th day of owning the car, she ran a red light and hit another auto. Her pride and joy was destroyed. Not just damaged, but "totaled." Fortunately, there were no serious injuries. Her liability insurance covered the damage she did to the other driver's car, but she was up the proverbial creek. No money and no car.

The moral of this story is why we even have such a thing as insurance to begin with. Insure what you cannot afford to lose. There is a solid case for not insuring a six-year-old $2,500 automobile, but only if you can afford the loss if you wreck it. If you can't afford the loss and can't afford the cost of insuring what you can't afford to lose, then you have no business being in the game in the first place.

Read on to find out what "full" coverage means. Find out how Chuck was well covered financially, and why he was not in the same financial bind as the fine young lady. Find out the difference between "liability" and "collision" insurance, and many other critical facts that you need to know about car insurance.

Life is full of risk, as both Chuck and the granddaughter found out. Some risks we are stuck with. Other risks can be transferred to someone else. For a price, we can shift some of our risks to insurance companies. So you need to know about insurance.

If you are ever going to own anything, you must know how to protect your property. On top of that, and maybe even more important, you have a responsibility to protect the rest of the world from any damage *you* may cause.

The big world of insurance can be very complicated. We stay with the basics here to keep things simple. If you don't learn the basics about the kinds of insurance you may need, sooner or later you may pay a very heavy price.

We do not cover everything about insurance. However, if you learn what's here, you will be off to a good start, and you will probably know more than a lot of people.

In 1898, there were about 100 cars on the road in the entire nation. That's a little hard for us to visualize, but it's true. Nobody worried much about two cars being in a wreck with each other. There were dangers nonetheless. The biggest risk was that a noisy car would scare a horse! While a few people had cars, the rest of the world was riding around in horse and buggies. A horse would often panic when one of the loud contraptions came down the street. The horse often would stampede in terror, dragging the buggy and its hapless occu-pants along with it. This kind of happening brought about the need for automobile insurance. The first policy was sold in the United States in 1898.

Things have changed. Now there are approximately 200 million cars on the road. That number, of course, includes Chuck's new car! It is estimated that American motorists drive over 2,000 trillion miles a year. How many trips to the sun and back would that represent?

One thing is certain. The automobile is the greatest danger to your life and to your pocketbook that you are ever likely to encounter. In a matter of seconds, a trip to get a hamburger can cost your life or someone else's life. Without adequate insur-ance, a moment of innocent carelessness can destroy you financially. Since all of us drive or ride in cars, we had better be glad there are insurance companies, even if we hate paying the premiums they charge.

For Chuck, buying the car was exciting and fun. But owning an auto is serious business. You see, having a car exposes you to a lot of risk. Not only is a car a fairly valuable asset, but it can be a source of harm to the owner and others in case of an accident. Fortunately, Chuck passed on most of that risk to an insurance company.

## The Different Kinds of Car Insurance

Here is where the confusion starts for most people. We have to know what kinds of car insurance coverage there are and what kind we need. There are many parts of insurance that go into the policy we buy. Each part insures us against different things.

### *Liability Insurance*

We start with the most important kind of car insurance. Liability insurance pays for injuries or damage that *you* may cause. The entire concept of liability is based on laws that say we each are responsible for our own actions. If we injure another person or cause damage to his or her property, we must compensate him or her. But how many of us can pay for thousands of dollars in property damage, or millions for loss of life? That's why we pay premiums to insurance companies. By doing so, we transfer the risk to the insurance company.

When you buy liability coverage as part of an auto insurance policy, you protect yourself—to the limits of the policy—in several ways. In return for your premium dollars, the insurance company agrees to stand good for you for accidental damage caused if:

- You are driving a vehicle named in the policy.

- You are driving someone else's car with his or her permission.

- Someone is driving your car with your permission.

Liability insurance also provides another very critical form of protection for you. The insurance company agrees to defend you in a lawsuit resulting from an accident someone claims you caused. This is only one more of many reasons you must never be without liability insurance.

Your liability insurance covers only damage you cause to other people or their property. It does not cover you or your car.

## Limits of Liability

When you buy liability coverage as part of an automobile insurance policy, you must select "limits" of coverage. Most policies have what are called "split-limits." These are expressed as "10/20/10" or "50/100/25." The numbers refer to thousands of dollars.

- The first figure is the limit the insurance company will pay for injuries per person in each accident;

- The second is the maximum total that will be paid for the injuries of two or more people for each accident; and

- The last figure applies to property damage.

In other words, if one person is hurt, the first figure is the most that the insurance company would pay. If more than one person is hurt in the same accident, the second figure is the limit of your insurance. So, if 10 people are hurt, that amount must cover all 10 injuries.

The laws of most states require each owner of a car to have a certain minimum amount of liability coverage, say 10/20/10. That's really not much coverage. If you cause $100,000 in injuries and you bought a low-limit policy, you are responsible for everything above the limits of the policy.

The amount of coverage you select affects your premium. Normally you can choose higher coverage for only a few dollars more than lower coverage would cost. We strongly recommend that you purchase more than the minimum amount the law requires. You should protect yourself with higher coverage.

### Uninsured Motorists Insurance

This part of an auto policy is often misunderstood. Under most terms and conditions, this part of a policy does not fix your car in case of an accident if the other driver doesn't have insurance. But, it will cover injuries to you and your passengers caused by another driver who does not have insurance, or by a hit-and-run driver. As with all forms of insurance, you choose the limits of coverage. Uninsured motorists coverage is a low-cost option in most policies. It usually makes good sense to add this when you buy a policy.

### Medical Payments Coverage

This one is pretty much what it says. If you choose this in your policy, you and anyone in your car are covered up to the set limits stated in the policy. This coverage pays for medical treatment of injuries resulting from the accident. It does not matter whose fault the accident is. This one even covers you if you are hit by a car while walking.

### Collision and Comprehensive

Now we come to the kind of insurance that pays for damage to or the loss of your car. If you finance your car, the lender will usually require you to purchase this kind of insurance. Just about every auto financing contract in the world requires you to keep the car covered with collision and comprehensive insurance until the loan is paid. Chuck's bank required him to have this coverage on the car that was financed for him. Lenders want to know that their collateral will be protected. You do not have to purchase insurance through the lender. You may purchase the coverage from someone other than the lender. That will often, if not always, be cheaper.

### Collision Insurance

This is the insurance that pays to fix your car if you have a wreck, whether it's your fault or not. There is no specified limit in the policy. Most policies will not pay for repairs that cost more than your car is worth. If the repairs exceed the value of the car, it is considered to be "totaled." An insurance company will not buy you a new car! Rather, the insurance company will pay you the value of the car at the time of the accident. If the car is financed, the check probably will be payable jointly to you and to the lender. You will have to settle up with the lender.

Remember in another chapter we warned about the dangers of financing an automobile for too long a term? Here is another example of that trap if you went for the low, low payments. You may owe $10,000 on a car that really is only worth $7,000 on the market. That doesn't hit you in the face if you are content to drive the car for a long time. But, were you to total the car in a wreck, the insurance company would only pay you $7,000. So, you still owe the creditor $3,000 and you are on foot! That is something to think about.

Collision insurance always has "deductibles." This means you are responsible for the damage up to the amount of the deductible you have chosen. The insurance kicks in for the loss in excess of the deductible. The lower the deductible, the higher the premium, and vice-versa. Deductibles you can choose may range from $50 to $1,000.

Again, no matter who is at fault, the insurance company will pay. However, if the other driver is at fault, he or she owes you for your deductible — if you can collect it.

You should always call your insurance agent or company and let someone there know if you have been in an accident. If the other driver is at fault and has insurance, you should file a claim against the other driver's insurance company. After all, you don't want your insurance to pay unless you can't collect from the other driver.

Your collision insurance will pay for your damages even if the other driver does not have insurance. Later, the insurance company will try to collect from the other driver. The company has that right. For the record, this is called "subrogation."

### Comprehensive Insurance

This is the coverage that pays for things other than an accident. This coverage protects your investment if your car is stolen or damaged by vandalism, if your windshield is broken, or even if your car catches fire and burns. Comprehensive coverage usually is very broad.

### Do You Need Collision and Comprehensive?

If your car is financed, that decision will be made by whomever granted you the credit to buy the car. If your car is paid for, then you have the choice. You have to weigh the cost of the insurance against the value of your car. You must consider your ability to pay for repairs yourself, or to replace the car if it is totaled. If the car is valuable and you don't have a lot of savings, then you better spring for the insurance. If it's a "rag" and you can afford to buy another one if it burns, maybe you would be better off taking a chance that you won't have a wreck. Put the premiums in the bank, and you may be ahead.

The general rule about this kind of decision is to take a chance only with what you are willing and able to lose.

### What to Do if You Have an Accident

First and foremost, do not admit any liability or fault. At the time of an accident, you may be upset and confused about the wreck. You really may not know if you are at fault or not. Don't jump out of the car yelling or accusing the other driver, either. The scene of an accident is not the place to get into an argument with the other driver.

The police should be called immediately. If there are injuries, tell the police that on the telephone. Assuming no one is hurt, wait for the police. You may want to exchange information, such as insurance policy information, with the other driver. Don't move your car until the police arrive and tell you to. Don't worry about who is at fault. Just tell the police officers the facts when they get there.

Afterwards, you should notify your insurance agent or company. Notifying the company is not the same as filing a claim. Even if the wreck is not your fault and the other driver has insurance, you should notify your insurance company. If you have trouble collecting from the other party, you can contact your insurance company again for help or to file a claim on your policy if that becomes necessary.

## Discounts on Your Insurance

Most companies offer many kinds of discounts. If you have picked a good agent, he or she will help you save the most money possible on your policy. Knowing these tips will help you get the most for your money.

- Good Driver Discounts—This is a discount for having a clean record. It means you've received no tickets for moving violations and no wrecks have been charged to you for the last three to five years.

- Economy Car Discount—Smaller cars cause less damage in an accident and are cheaper to repair. Therefore, they cost less to insure.

- Good Student Discounts—These are for the bright (or hard-working) students who get good grades, usually a "B" average or better.

- Drivers Education Discounts—Most companies will give a discount for anyone who has completed or who is taking a Drivers Education course. These are taught in most high schools. Drivers Ed can also be taken by any driver at a commercial school.

- Multi-Auto Discounts—Most companies will give a discount if you own and insure two or more cars with the same company. Sometimes, depending on the company and on how the cars are licensed, one car can be a student's and the other can be Dad's. They both must be in the same household and located at the same place.

- Low Mileage Discount—If you don't drive a lot of miles in a year, you may be able to get a discount.

Ask your insurance agent or company about any other discount that may be available.

**What Is an "Assigned Risk"?**

This is what happens to you if you don't qualify for regular insurance. You go into a "pool." Your application for insurance is assigned to a company on a rotating basis. Each insurance company is obligated to accept "assigned risk" applications based on a complicated formula governed by the state. These policies carry much higher premiums.

You get put into a pool when you have too many wrecks or get too many traffic tickets. Generally, after so many years of a good record, anyone in the "assigned risk" program can get out and qualify for regular rates again.

Keep your record clean, because you don't want to have to pay high premiums. You don't want to be an "assigned risk."

**A Word of Caution**

You wouldn't lend thousands of dollars to people whom you really don't know well, or couldn't prove were good risks, would you? Just because they smile at you and promise that they will repay you is not enough. You would check them out, just like any lender would before making a loan. You want to know about their ability to repay you and about their reputation.

Yet, people often buy auto insurance without first checking the reputation and financial condition of the insurance company. When you buy any type of insurance policy, you pay money to the company in exchange for a promise that the company will pay you if it becomes required under the terms of the policy. It's much like a loan transaction. You are actually extending credit (your trust) to them! So you'd better be careful about selecting an insurance company.

There are some fly-by-night outfits around. In a number of states, including Louisiana and Alabama, some big operations have gone "belly-up" in recent years. They took in a lot of premium dollars, but that money seems to have disappeared. When claims started piling up, the policy holders didn't get paid! Those companies have been shut down, but thousands of people may never get their money. In only the two states we mentioned, one company alone failed to pay out millions of dollars in valid claims that were owed to people.

Let the buyer beware! You should check out any insurance company before you sign a policy contract or make a payment. Policyholders may avoid a loss simply by calling their state insurance commission and requesting a report on their insurance company. Better Business Bureaus, too, often have files on any insurance companies who fail to pay claims satisfactorily. Do business only with reputable agents and companies — ones that have a proven and solid track record.

## THINGS TO REMEMBER

*Auto Liability Insurance* protects you from the claims of others you may injure or whose property you may damage. Each of us is responsible for damage we cause to the property of others or for injury to people. Liability insurance does not pay for damages to your car.

Make sure your limits of liability are adequate. Higher limits cost very little more than low ones.

*Uninsured Motorists Insurance* normally covers *only* injury to you or your passengers if the other party does not have insurance. It does not cover your car.

*Auto Comprehensive and Collision Insurance* protects *your* property, no matter who is at fault. You will be protected even if the other person does not have insurance. This insurance does not cover your responsibility to anyone else if you have an accident.

When your car is an older one with little value, you should consider not carrying collision.

If you have an accident, do not admit liability, and do not be unpleasant or get into an argument. Call the police immediately.

There are often discounts on car insurance.

*Assigned Risk* is a pool of insurance for people who do not qualify under normal conditions. It is expensive.

# Chapter Thirteen

# Other Kinds of Insurance

Chuck Taylor is relatively young. He's not married, and besides his car loan, he doesn't owe much money. He has protected his automobile investment with collision and comprehensive insurance. In addition, he has protected himself with liability coverage. Sales people contact him frequently trying to sell him other insurance. They will be calling you, too, before long, if they haven't already. You need to have a grip on the basics of life insurance and other kinds of insurance.

## Life Insurance

Life insurance has been around for a long time in one form or another. Today, more than $5 trillion worth of life insurance is in force in the United States. That's a five with 12 zeros on the end!

*Life Insurance Provides for the Financial Security of Those People Who Depend on Your Income*

There are different kinds of life insurance policies. We limit this discussion to the two most common — whole life and term life. Life insurance pays to the named beneficiary when the insured person dies. The basic purpose of life insurance is to provide for the financial security of family members who depended on the income of the insured person during his or her life.

### Whole Life

If someone dies during the period of coverage, the insurance company pays the face value of a policy to the beneficiary. If premiums are paid long enough, then "cash value" will build up and will be paid if the policy is "cashed in," even before death. The insured person can even borrow this cash value. It can also be used to pay premiums to keep the insurance in force when income is lost or reduced.

Remember one basic fact. A whole life policy, no matter what it is called, is an investment product combined with insurance protection. Whole life insurance is much more expensive than term insurance, which we explain a little later. There is nothing wrong with your choosing this kind of combination investment and insurance, but you should take the time to understand the choices and the costs of this kind of insurance policy.

There are many "spinoffs" of this basic kind of policy. They are known by a lot of names. Many of them are very similar. All are designed to attract and compete for your insurance dollar. The facts you have learned about our free enterprise market economy apply here also. We have a lot of choices to make — and we have the responsibility to ourselves to learn how to make them.

### Term Insurance

This is the simplest and cheapest of all life insurance policies. For a given premium and for as long as you pay it according to terms, you get a certain amount of life insurance.

If you die while the policy is in force, your beneficiary gets paid. If you cancel the policy or stop paying the premiums, you or your beneficiary get nothing. With term insurance you pay a low price specifically to provide some money for a loved one if you die. Term insurance comes in many forms, but the concept is the same for each form. Many employers offer term insurance as an employee benefit.

Premiums for all life insurance policies are governed by the type of policy, your age, your health, and sometimes even your occupation. Often there is a discount if you don't smoke, because evidence shows that non-smokers live longer. Also, premiums for women may be cheaper than for men. Data show that women live longer. Also, if you have certain kinds of dangerous hobbies, insurance premiums could be higher.

A note here about beneficiaries. Our lives change, often in many ways. As only one example, a young, single person may obtain some form of life insurance and make his or her parents the beneficiary. Later, he or she gets married, but forgets that the parents are still beneficiary. You should always remember to change your insurance beneficiary as necessary. That way the person you wish will get the money, should something happen to you.

There are many, many more details about life insurance, but now you know the most important facts. Find a trustworthy, knowledgeable agent to help you. But remember that the agent gets a commission on all the insurance that he or she can sell you.

## Medical or Health Insurance

When Chuck was a little younger, he thought he was invincible. He never thought about getting sick or having a serious injury. Chuck didn't think much about health insurance. When he got a good job that had health benefits provided for him, he still didn't think much about it. But a young friend at work was seriously injured in a car wreck. He was in the

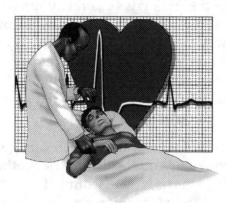

*Lack of Health Insurance Can Be Expensive*

hospital nearly two weeks. When he was back at work, he told Chuck that, without insurance, he would have been ruined financially. Chuck began to realize that, if it could happen to a friend, it could happen to him.

Medical or health insurance pays all or part of doctor bills and hospital charges if you get sick or injured in an accident. In some policies, other miscellaneous medical expenses, such as ambulance service, are covered as well. Some policies may even cover part of the costs of treatment for mental health. The cost of health care in recent years has soared, and without good health insurance, an illness could wipe out a person financially.

The need for public access to affordable health care is of great national concern. Many people do not have any medical insurance. They are often unable to pay for needed treatment. This tends to overburden charity health systems, funded by our tax dollars. There is a strong push by some to create some form of socialized medicine. But, as with any problem, there are no solutions, only difficult choices.

Health insurance may cover part or all of necessary expenses for treatment of four main areas: hospitalization, surgery, doctor visits, and major medical expenses resulting from long or severe illness or injury. Most policies will have deductibles and co-insurance requirements. A deductible is an amount you must pay before the insurance takes over. Co-insurance means that the insurance company pays a percentage (usually 80 percent) of costs, and you pay the remaining percentage.

Chuck, however, belongs to an HMO (Health Maintenance Organization) through his employer, as a part of his job benefits. HMOs usually are not insurance companies. HMOs are organizations made up of enrolled doctors, hospitals, and other health care providers. Chuck pays only $10 each time he needs medical care, whether it is a doctor visit, emergency treatment, or hospitalization. He must normally, however, go to a doctor or provider who is a member of that HMO. This kind of health care program can be excellent, but often expensive. A set monthly amount is paid to the HMO, much the same as if it were an insurance premium. Chuck got a job with excellent benefits, and his employer pays most of this monthly amount. He is very lucky because most part-time workers do not get such benefits. His employer clearly wants to hire Chuck full-time when he graduates from college.

Most medical and health insurance is provided through group policies. Employers arrange this coverage with insurance companies and provide some or all of the premium cost as a benefit to the employee. Self-employed people, or those who work at a business which does not provide medical insurance, must purchase an individual policy if they wish coverage.

Under many circumstances, insurance companies will require that you take a medical examination before they will provide you coverage. This is true not only for health insurance, but often for life insurance also. If the tests indicate that you have AIDS or that you use illegal drugs, it is almost impossible for you to get a policy. In the case of group policies, arranged by employers, there may be provision for enrollment without a physical.

## Health and Accident Insurance

This insurance, usually called H&A, is very limited in coverage and benefits. It must not be confused with true health insurance described in previous examples. The policies are often low-cost, but pay limited amounts only for specified occurrences. They will rarely even begin to cover the full cost of treatment. They may, for example, pay you $75 per day if you are hospitalized for a covered event. This won't go far. Hospital stays can easily exceed $1,000 or more per day. Health and accident insurance is aggressively promoted by mail. Frequently, you will receive mail urging you to buy this insurance.

## Residential or Property Insurance

This kind of insurance offers protection to people who own their homes. It also can be bought by someone renting an apartment or a home. In the first case, the insurance includes protection for personal property and the value of the home. In the second case, it covers the tenant's (renter's) personal property. Both types usually include liability insurance or personal protection. This very important protection will cover you if your dog bites somebody, or if somebody falls and is injured while visiting you. This liability insurance is usually very broad in coverage and very important to have. This liability insurance does not cover your car. That must be separate.

We are not going into any more detail about this kind of insurance, because there are so many different coverages and options. When you first get an apartment, find a good insurance agent who will explain your choices. Just ask him or her questions. If the agent doesn't make you comfortable with the answers, find another agent.

When the time comes to buy your first home, the mortgage company will require you to have homeowners insurance to protect its mortgage.

## Other Kinds of Insurance

There are other kinds of insurance, such as disability insurance, credit life insurance, and mortgage cancellation insurance (which is a type of credit life insurance). Unless you go to work in the insurance business, you will never learn about all kinds of policies! There are so many. As you go through life, learn how to ask questions and protect yourself. And do business only with reputable people and companies. If you put the information about insurance we have provided to good use, you will make wiser decisions than many people are able to do.

## THINGS TO REMEMBER

Life insurance is primarily designed to benefit your loved ones and family members who are dependent upon your income.

Term life policies offer insurance on your life at low premiums, while whole life insurance combines forms of investment with the insurance.

Health insurance can be critically important and often can be arranged with group policies through employee benefit programs.

Health care costs in the United States are rising dramatically and are a national concern.

Property insurance can be purchased both by homeowners and renters to cover personal belongings from fire, theft, and other causes of loss.

Take the initiative to make sure an insurance company is reputable and financially sound. The time to do this is *before* you sign a contract or pay a premium.

# Chapter Fourteen

# You and the IRS

Chuck Taylor still remembers his very first payday during the first summer that he worked. He was excited, to put it mildly. He could hardly wait to get that fat paycheck in his hands. Chuck was making $4.25 an hour at the time, and he had been able to work 92 hours that two-week pay period. He had done his figuring and knew that check would be $416.50, counting the overtime pay. Chuck had plans for that money.

But what a shock! When he got his check, it was only for $338.64. His employer had held out $31.86 for FICA (Social Security tax and Medicare), and $46 for federal income tax. Had the bookkeeper made a mistake? No. Chuck had simply forgotten about deductions for federal income tax and Social Security tax. Chuck had heard of these things before, but really never associated them with himself until now. Chuck asked the bookkeeper about these deductions from his paycheck. The bookkeeper told Chuck that when he filled out his W-4, he had claimed zero dependents. Well, Chuck had thought since he wasn't married and had no children, he didn't have any dependents! That was a few years ago, and Chuck has learned a lot about taxes since. You will also learn these things as you read this chapter.

Laws require that, in nearly all cases, an employer take out these taxes. This is called "withholding." Most workers have to pay federal income taxes and, in many states, state income taxes also. Later in this chapter you will learn more about when and how much.

Our tax laws are so complicated that even the experts are confused. But, fear not! In this book we cover only the bare bones about taxes. These are important facts. Nobody wants to get into trouble with Uncle Sam. But, tens of thousands of people do because they never learned a few simple things. We're not talking about tax cheats, but about honest people who didn't know what they should have known.

We have said before in this book that a lot about life isn't fair, and that includes taxes. Most people feel they have to pay too much in taxes because the government wastes money. Maybe that's true, but we can't help you there. Don't forget that without taxes, we wouldn't even have roads or bridges, let alone the many valuable services government provides.

This chapter does not try to teach you how to save money on taxes. We stick to informing you of certain responsibilities that you have.

The subject of taxes is one that we probably all would like to ignore. But taxes are a reality of life, and the Internal Revenue Service (IRS) is the biggest and most important player in the game. The IRS is part of the federal government, and it collects taxes under laws passed by Congress. Federal income tax laws won't go away. We might as well make our life a little easier by learning something about them.

In this book, we have often referred to the reality that there is no such thing as something for nothing. Another fact of life is that all of us sometimes tend to take things for granted. When the Earth was created, there were no roads or bridges. Life was pretty tough. Later, what we now call civilization got started. When that happened, so did taxes.

In a civilized society, we have governments. Governments are expected to provide services people cannot provide for themselves. Like it or not, every civilization has had to have armies to defend itself against enemies. All reasonable people agree that we need things such as roads, bridges, schools, libraries, disaster relief, national parks, and so on. Add to that list things we wish we didn't need, but do, such as a congress to make laws, courts to enforce and interpret those laws, and useful and effective social programs to help those less able to help themselves. It all adds up to the fact that government must have a stream of income with which to provide these things. Much of the federal government's income comes from taxes on the earnings of workers. In other words, the federal government takes money from people who work. The government then spends that money as directed by Congress.

All we have tried to do so far in this chapter is to help rationalize why we have to pay taxes. We don't have to like it! Next, we give you some easy-to-learn facts about the income tax laws that affect you. If you take the time to learn these basics, you and the IRS may get along better. As we describe the things that follow, we are forced to use some fairly precise words because we are dealing with tax laws.

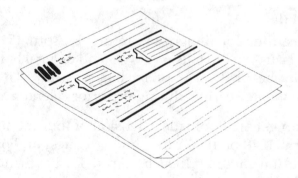

## What Is a Tax Return?

A tax return is a form that the taxpayer fills out and sends to the IRS each year. It can be one of several forms which we explain later. Each completed tax form contains income and other information that must be supplied to the government. In the U.S., taxpayers provide their own information on these forms. But the IRS also collects a variety of data to ensure that taxpayers cannot easily cheat. The IRS is able to check up on what taxpayers report on their forms.

The purpose of the tax return is to compute the amount of income tax that the taxpayer owes for the period covered by the return.

## Who Must File an IRS Return?

If you are a U.S. citizen or a foreign citizen who lives in the U.S. *and* have income above a certain amount, you must file a return. For example, in 1995 the income levels above which individuals must file a return were as follows. These numbers are scheduled to rise each year in order to compensate for inflation, so remember to check for the proper figures for any other year other than 1995.

| | |
|---|---|
| Single . . . . . . . . . . . . . . . . . . . . . . . . . . . . . . . . . . . . | $6,400 |
| Married and filing a separate return . . . . . . . . | $2,500 |
| Married and filing a joint return . . . . . . . . . . . | $11,550 |
| Filing as "Head of Houshold" . . . . . . . . . . . . . | $8,250 |

## When to File

The deadline for filing a tax return is April 15 for most individuals. If April 15 falls on a weekend or legal holiday, the return may be filed on the next business day. That return covers the income earned during the prior calendar year.

You can get an automatic extension of four months to file either Form 1040 or 1040A by filing a request on Form 4868. This extension must be filed by April 15. Payment for any estimated taxes due must be paid when the extension is filed. Otherwise, there will be penalties and interest.

## Where to File

Returns are filed with the Internal Revenue Service Center for the region where you live. A list of filing locations is provided in the instruction booklet for Forms 1040 and 1040A provided by the IRS.

## What Form to Use

Most people use one of three principal forms: Forms 1040, 1040A, and 1040EZ.

Only single or married filing jointly taxpayers with no dependents, and under age 65, may use Form 1040EZ. It's the shortest and easiest to use.

Form 1040A is a two-page form accompanied by a two-page Schedule 1. You may use 1040A if you do not itemize deductions and if your income consists only of wages, salaries, tips, taxable scholarships and fellowships, unemployment compensation, pensions, annuities, IRAs, Social Security, railroad retirement benefits, dividends, and interest. Also, your taxable income must be less than $50,000 under the law in effect in 1995.

Any taxpayer whose needs or circumstances are other than those above should file using Form 1040.

## What Is Taxable Income?

Taxable income is "Adjusted Gross Income"(AGI) minus allowances for deductions and exemptions. Adjusted gross income is simply your total income from all sources, less special deductions such as alimony paid, IRA contributions, or reimbursed employee expenses. Deductions can include such things as local property taxes, charitable contributions, and, in some cases, medical expenses.

Child support is not deductible by the person who pays it. Nor is it taxable to the person receiving it. Alimony is deductible by the person who pays it, and it is taxable to the person who receives it if it is paid because of court rulings.

## What Is a Standard Deduction?

All taxpayers are entitled to a "Standard Deduction," whether they itemize deductions or not. The amount depends upon whether you are married, single, or a "head of household."

Standard deduction amounts for 1995 were as follows. (Remember, these, too, are scheduled to change each year.)

Single . . . . . . . . . . . . . . . . . . . . . . . . . . . . . . . . .   $3,900

Married and filing jointly* . . . . . . . . . . . . . . . .   $6,550

Married filing separately. . . . . . . . . . . . . . . . .   $3,275

Filing as head of houshold . . . . . . . . . . . . . . .   $5,750

   * If one spouse files separately, the other cannot itemize.

These amounts simply represent income which is not subject to income taxes.

### What Is an "Exemption"?

The full name is "personal exemption," or "dependency exemption," whichever the case. This is an amount that you can deduct from your gross income, lowering your taxable income. The amount for 1995 was $2,500 for each eligible exemption. This amount is adjusted annually to reflect the inflation rate. The IRS announces the adjusted amount each year.

Exemptions, like deductions, represent income on which you do not have to pay taxes.

### Who Is a Dependent?

A dependent is someone for whom you provide the majority of support, and for whom you may claim a dependency deduction from your taxable income. You probably don't have any dependents right now! But someday you will, so read on. There are five tests that must be met to determine if you may claim a person as a dependent on your tax return. They are as follows:

1. The person must have less than $2,500 gross income for the year; unless the dependent is your child and either is under the age of 19 or is a full-time student under the age of 24.

*If a child earned over $2,500* and meets the age or student rule, he or she may be claimed as a dependent on his or her parent's return only if he or she *does not* claim himself or herself as a dependent on his/her own taxes and raise the child's. However, the child's tax rates are usually much lower.

You may have to read the above a couple of times to figure it out, but this is an important rule. The effect can be to lower a parent's tax rate and raise the child's. However, the child's tax rates are usually much lower.

2. Over one-half of the dependent's support must have been furnished by the taxpayer. This situation is usually encountered when a taxpayer is taking care of a parent or relative, and the person has income to provide part of his or her own support.

   In the case of children of divorced or separated parents, the general rule is that the custodial parent gets the deduction, unless stated otherwise in a child-support or separation agreement.

3. The person must fall within one of the following relationships:

   (a) Son or daughter, grandchild, great grandchild, stepchild, or adopted child

   (b) Brother or sister

   (c) Brother or sister by the half blood

   (d) Stepbrother or stepsister

   (e) Mother or father, ancestor of either

   (f) Stepfather or stepmother

   (g) Nephew or niece

   (h) Aunt or uncle

     (i)  Generally, an in-law

     (j)  A person who is a live-in, as long as the relationship does not violate local law and as long as that person lived with you the entire year.

  4. The dependent must not have filed a joint return with his or her spouse. We think this says that a "friend" whom you support cannot be claimed as a dependent on your return if he or she files a joint return with a legal husband or wife!

  5. The dependent must be a citizen, national, or resident of the United States, Canada, or Mexico. There are a few other conditions relative to this rule if the person is not a citizen.

## Who Is a "Head of Household"?

Married couples filing joint returns receive somewhat more favorable treatment on tax rates than single people. To help offset this, the IRS provides a "Head of Household" filing category, with lower tax rates than the usual "single" filer.

To qualify as Head of Household, a taxpayer must not be married at the close of the tax year or must have lived separately from his or her spouse during the last six months of the year. In addition, the taxpayer must maintain as his or her home a household which is the principal place where one or more of the following lived for at least half of the year:

  1. A son or daughter, a grandchild, an adopted child, or a stepchild or foster child. If one of these is a foster child or is married at the close of the tax year, he or she must meet other dependency tests.

  2. Any other relative eligible to be claimed as a dependent, *except* those eligible to be claimed under a multiple support agreement.

3. Your father or mother may live separately from you if you pay more than one-half of the cost of keeping up their main home. How to better say it???

## Who Must Have a Social Security Number?

Any dependent over one year old that you are eligible to claim on your return must have a Social Security number. That number must be entered on the tax return.

A Social Security number is issued by the government. To work, you must have such a number. Your Social Security number is used in reporting and recording tax information, and the government also uses it for other purposes.

## What Is the Difference Between "Tax Liability" and "Withholding"?

Every time you are paid, your employer withholds some federal tax from your paycheck. This withholding will almost never equal your tax "liability" for the year. The amount your employer withholds each payday is determined by the W-4 form you fill out when you start your job. Your actual tax liability (the total amount of tax you must pay for the year) is determined by the results of completing your tax return. In completing your return, you count all of your income and take your deductions. These calculations determine your taxable income. Your actual tax for the year is based on this figure from tax tables provided you by the IRS.

There are many circumstances that can cause your withholdings for the year to be too much or too little. If too much of your money was withheld from your earnings during the year, you can get a refund when you file your tax return. If not enough money was withheld from your earnings, you owe more taxes that must be paid when you file your tax return form.

**What Is a "W-2"?**

This is a form that employers are required to complete for every employee they had during the year. You get three copies: one for your records, one to file with your federal tax return, and one to file with any state or local tax return that may be required. The original goes to the IRS so that it will know how much income you had. That way the tax officials will know to expect you to file a tax return. You should get a W-2 for each job that you held during a year. The amount of wages shown on W-2s and any other income must be included in your gross income on your tax return.

**What Is a "1099"?**

A W-2 is used for reporting income from normal wages. But there are other kinds of income you may receive, such as interest or dividends. If so, that income may be reported on what is called a "1099." There are many versions of a 1099, and each is for a different kind of income. Each has a different suffix. The most common are a 1099-G (for unemployment benefits), a 1099-INT (for interest income of more than $10), or a 1099-MISC (for miscellaneous income). If you receive a 1099-MISC for work that you have performed and no Social Security tax was withheld, you may be required to pay that Social Security tax along with your income tax.

You will receive a 1099 if you receive income from any other source which the law requires to be reported. That income must be declared on your tax return.

**What Is a "W-4"?**

This is really a simple form, but one that is often misunderstood. When you are hired in a regular job, the employer is required by law to withhold income taxes. The amount of tax the employer is required to withhold from your pay is determined by the W-4 the employer will give you to fill out.

A W-4 form has only a few blanks to fill out and complete instructions on how to do it. The purpose of the form is to help you know how many "allowances" to claim and what your filing "status" (married, single, etc.) will be. An allowance is similar to an exemption, except that when your employer refers to tax tables, the status and number of allowances will tell him or her how much tax must be withheld from your pay. Your money that is withheld is sent to the federal government by your employer.

The more allowances you are entitled to claim, the less tax will be withheld from your pay. If you do not claim as many allowances as you are entitled to, too much tax will be taken out. When you file your tax return, you will get a refund. You will have let the government use some of your money during the year interest free.

If you have income only from one source, completing a W-4 is really easy. The form asks you if you are married or single, your name, address, and Social Security number, and how many allowances you are claiming. You are asked simple questions that tell you the number of allowances. Normally, you get one allowance for each dependent.

If you are married and your spouse is working, or you have other income, or pay child care expenses, allowances can change. But again, the instructions are fairly clear.

Completing a W-4 correctly can be very important. If too much tax is withheld, you can always get it back. If you claim too many allowances and not enough of your money is held out as taxes, you will owe more money when you file your return. Sometimes, there can be additional penalties plus interest if you owe too much tax at the end of the year.

**Income Tax Rates**

In the U.S. we have a progressive tax rate structure. That simply means that, as your taxable income goes up above certain levels, you move into a higher tax rate bracket. In other words, you pay one tax rate on a certain amount of taxable income, and a higher rate on an additional amount of taxable income. Therefore, you pay a bigger percentage of your income to the federal government as your income grows.

For taxable income received during 1995, the brackets and rates were as follows. (Remember, these brackets, and perhaps the rates, change each year—so the numbers below refer to 1995 only.)

### For Single Taxpayers

If your taxable income is less than $23,350, the tax rate is 15 percent.

If your taxable income is between $23,350 and $56,550, the tax is $3,502.50 plus 28 percent of the amount over $23,350.

If your taxable income is between $56,550 and $117,950, the tax is $12,798.50 plus 31 percent of the amount over $56,550.

If your taxable income is between $117,950 and $256,500, the tax is $31,832.50 plus 36 percent of the amount over $117,950.

If your taxable income exceeds $256,500, the tax is $81,710.50 plus 39.6 percent of the amount over $256,500.

### For Married Taxpayers Filing Jointly

If your taxable income is less than $39,000, the tax rate is 15 percent.

If your taxable income is between $39,000 and $94,250, the tax is $5,850 plus 28 percent of the amount over $39,000.

If your taxable income is between $94,250 and $143,600, the tax is $21,320 plus 31 percent on the amount over $94,250.

If your taxable income is between $143,600 and $256,000, the tax is $36,618.50 plus 36 percent on the amount over $143,600.

If your taxable income exceeds $256,000, the tax is $77,262.50 plus 39.6 percent on the amount over $256,000.

As you study the above taxable amounts and rates, two facts become obvious about the current tax laws. First, people earning a higher income pay a larger share of their taxable income to the federal government. Second, our wise people in Washington feel that married people should pay higher tax rates!

## What Is a "Tax Credit"?

A tax credit is not the same as a deduction. A deduction is an amount you can deduct from your *taxable* income. You pay taxes on the rest. A tax credit is something you can actually subtract from the final taxes you owe to the government. Think about this a little, and you will see the big difference.

## What Is "Earned Income Credit (EIC)"?

This fearsome expression is fairly simple (although nothing is really simple about tax laws). If you qualify for an Earned Income Credit, believe it or not, you can actually get something for nothing.

The EIC is a special tax credit for certain workers. It reduces the tax you owe, or may give you a refund even if you don't owe any tax. The credit for 1994 was as much as $306 if you didn't have a qualifying child and were at least 25 years old. (As of this writing, the 1995 IRS rules had not yet been issued.) If you had one qualifying child, the credit could have been as much as $2,038. If you had more than one qualifying child, it was as much as $2,528. If you had a qualifying child and could take the credit, you had to fill in and attach Schedule EIC to your return.

The EIC was *designed* to give people an incentive to work and keep them off the welfare rolls. However, like many federal programs, it has expanded greatly and is often used by some people to receive money from the government for little work.

## Special Notes About Taxes

If your income (under 1995 law) was under $6,250 and you were single, you were not even required to file a tax return. *However,* if taxes were held out from your paychecks, you must file a return to get those taxes refunded to you. Otherwise, the IRS keeps your money.

If you file a 1040EZ or a 1040, all you have to do is enter your name and address, Social Security number, attach your W-2s, sign the return, and send it in. The IRS will figure everything else for you. If you have a refund coming, you will get it. If you owe more, you will get a bill.

Some young people and their parents can get in a jam over this. They don't communicate; so the young person claims himself or herself as a dependent, and so does Mom and/or Dad. This is a "no-no." The same person cannot be claimed on two returns. In fact, if you *can be* claimed as a dependent by someone else, you cannot claim yourself as a dependent.

Each year thousands of taxpayers unnecessarily pay fees to a "tax service" when they could easily file their own return. In the case of a 1040EZ or a 1040A, the IRS will do the work for you free. The 1040EZ has only five lines to complete, but there are people who will not even look at it. They take it somewhere and pay a fee. We hope this book has taught you enough not to be one of these.

Many people also pay a fee to get their refund immediately rather than waiting a few weeks to receive it from the IRS. They pay a very high fee, or interest rate, for this. It is generally a very poor and costly practice. Also, it is a sign that people have not learned how to make smart decisions. Watch out for this type of advertisement or offer. Make sure you get the facts before making a decision that costs you money for very little benefit.

Chuck Taylor is never very happy when he has to pay his federal income taxes. Yet he realizes that the government provides some important things for him and for all people. That new car he is driving wouldn't go very far without streets and highways! So, he pays his taxes like every good citizen. But also like a good citizen, he is learning to pay attention to the people running for elected offices. He is learning that what politicians stand for and what they do will affect him. He is registered to vote, and does so. He makes a real effort to learn about candidates for office and cast an intelligent vote. He doesn't want his money that he pays in taxes wasted by poor management, bad laws, and wasteful programs. Chuck invites you to care about, and work for, good and honest government. That's your civic responsibility.

You have a stake in how the government spends its (your) money. You are paying taxes in one form or another — even if you do not have a job earning a paycheck. At the very least, every time you make a purchase, you are paying sales taxes. If you have a job and are earning money, you are paying Social Security taxes. If your earnings are enough to have taxable income, you are also paying income tax. So, you should care what the government does with the money you give to it.

Recently there has been a tremendous amount of discussion about reducing the size of the federal government. In the fall of 1994, enough Republicans were elected to give them a majority in both the House and Senate. For the prior 40 years, the Democrats have been in total control of both houses. Most of these Republicans campaigned on promises to reduce government. In fact, many signed the so-called "Contract With America." This document made a number of promises relating to streamlining government and making it more efficient. This relates to lowering taxes, balancing the federal government's budget, and so on.

All of this sounds good. Wouldn't you and your parents like to pay less in taxes? There are, however, serious problems to accomplishing all of these good things. We have something called "entitlement programs" in America. In general, these are programs which take tax money and transfer it to certain groups of people, generally lower income people. The largest of these are Social Security, Medicare, and Medicaid, but there are many more such programs. These entitlement programs, combined with the interest payments on the national debt — the money the government has borrowed in the past so that it could spend more than it collected in taxes — eat up 70 percent of the federal budget. Defense spending is only 19 percent. This means everything else the government spends is only 12 percent of the budget. Now you can get an idea of how little is spent on roads and bridges! It will be impossible to make meaningful inroads on reducing what the government spends without cutting entitlement programs.

If the politicians really attempt to cut entitlement programs, there will be a great amount of hollering and screaming and crying "foul." It will be painful. It is not our purpose to take sides on this issue, but to point out some facts to you. All through this book we have attempted to help you understand that there is no such thing as a free lunch. As you take your place in our economic system as a taxpayer, you will have to decide for yourself how you feel about such things.

Our system of taxation attempts to perform what is known as "social engineering." In other words, the federal government attempts not only to raise the tax revenue it feels it should or must have, but it also tries to shape other elements of our lives. Our tax code penalizes some things and encourages others. For example, permitting taxpayers to deduct mortgage interest tends to encourage home ownership. As another example, our progressive rate structure taxes higher-income people at a higher tax rate. This tends to discourage some workers from making the effort necessary to earn more money. The trouble with this kind of politics is that, as the politicians attempt to do one kind of good, they can do another kind of harm.

In 1995, one of the hottest topics in Congress and on the radio and TV talk shows was overhauling the entire concept of how we pay taxes. As you have learned in this chapter, we currently have what is called a "progressive" tax structure. Not only do you pay more taxes if you earn more, but you pay an *even higher rate* of taxes. Some people are pushing a "flat" tax. This would mean that everyone would pay the same rate of tax on the income they earn. This is not a new idea, but in 1995, the flat tax idea was being supported more widely. There are always two sides to a story. The supporters of a flat tax claim that, not only is it inherently more fair, but that it would encourage productivity, encourage people to work harder, and encourage people to earn more. They claim that the current system is a disincentive for people to make more money. The other side claims higher-income people *should* pay disproportionately higher taxes to subsidize those who earn less. Which philosophy has more merit? Beauty is often in the eyes of the beholder!

**As the Old Saying Goes, There Are
Only Two Things We Can Be Sure of in
Life — Death and Taxes!**

# Summary

In writing this book, we learned a lot. The meetings, the discussions, comparing notes, consulting other people for ideas, gathering information, looking up things we weren't sure about, and the discipline of organizing and doing the writing — all of these things and more taught both of us a lot.

Here were two people that saw and felt a need to make practical information about money and credit available to young adults who wanted to learn. One of us has spent his entire career teaching banking and finance; the other has spent over half of his life working with people in financial trouble, often because they didn't learn some of the things covered in this book when they were young. When this project started, we both thought we pretty much knew it all. Well, we are telling you that we didn't. Writing this book helped us realize that.

We hope you have gotten something worthwhile out of it also. We hope it is something that will stay with you through life and will one day reward you. There was a lot we couldn't cover in these pages. There is just so much to learn about life and money. In this day and age, the two have become closely connected — maybe too much so.

Not many of us live on farms anymore. We don't grow what we eat ourselves, nor do we spend much of our time on basic survival activities just to stay alive. Our economic and social structure has evolved into something that is complex. We do and make things for other people, and they do and make things for us. This leaves us no choice but to use a medium of exchange — money. We exchange our labor and talents for money. Then we use it to buy the things we need and, to the degree we can afford them, things we want.

Those of you who master the use of your money, that unit of measure of your labor and talent, will grow and prosper. Less of your earning power will be wasted on mistakes. More of it will be wisely invested in a better standard of living. Some are slaves to their money. That is sad and a waste. Their money should be their slave—a tool to use wisely and treat with respect.

Credit has become indispensable in our social and economic structure. As we approach the next century, it will be even more so. There are changes taking place, even as you read this, that will benefit those who build good credit and prove that they are responsible. Many of those changes are going to leave others behind, totally out of the race.

In today's market, currency is used much less than it was before. In the next ten years, it will be used even less. Fewer and fewer employers will hand out paychecks. Your earnings will be directly deposited into a financial institution. So, you say, you can just write a check. Writing checks is rapidly becoming out-dated. Credit cards and debit cards are here to stay, and even more important and exciting tools are on the way. So-called "smart cards" and "electronic money" will reduce the importance of checks and currency.

You will have to learn to use those tools. The best of them will require proof of responsibility—proof that you can manage your resources and your business correctly. People who can't, or won't, will be left behind.

We hope we have had a positive influence on your thinking about yourself and your role in the marketplace. Money doesn't grow on trees, and everyone cannot have everything he or she wants. You cannot expect the government to take care of you. We hope you have learned something about setting goals and going after them. Your life and your future are your responsibility. Take care of them.

So how do you manage? How do you get the things you need and want? How do you make the most of the money we make? Since there are no easy solutions, what are the answers?

Experience, learning, and the application of common sense mixed with some self-discipline are the answers. Experience takes time, but you have the opportunity to learn a lot right here in this book. Common sense is the application of experience and learning. Self-discipline is the tough part. None of us want to wait or be patient for what we want. But self-discipline is a trait that can be learned.

You have finished this book, and you haven't discovered any magic tricks. And you're not going to in life, either. We've shared with you a wealth of knowledge and experience, and there's more to come in your life. Be open to it. Go for it!

# Appendix A

# Federal Laws That Affect Consumers

In this section, we discuss the most important laws about credit that affect consumers. We are not going into the details or legal technicalities. If you were ever to need more complete information, the library or perhaps a lawyer can help.

## Truth In Lending

This law requires creditors to inform you of the cost of credit in terms of *"APR,"* or "Annual Percentage Rate." Basically, this is an "equalizer" and prevents a creditor from using a method of calculating interest that makes the interest rate sound lower that it actually is. Also, it requires a creditor to tell you when the interest starts. In the case of credit cards, which are a form of "open-end" credit, the law requires a creditor to tell you how the finance charges will be applied against the balance you owe. In other words, will there be a grace period? Will interest be charged against the average balance during the month, against the highest balance, or against the balance at the beginning of the cycle?

## Equal Credit Opportunity Act

This law prohibits discrimination in the granting of credit because of sex, race, color, marital status, religion, national origin, age, or because a person receives public assistance. Don't misunderstand this law. A creditor can "turn down" any credit application that does not meet credit criteria. Creditors simply cannot include any of the above things in their policies.

**Fair Credit Billing Act**

This law requires creditors, such as credit card issuers, to explain your rights if you are incorrectly charged on your credit account. The law sets forth what rights you have.

**Fair Credit Reporting Act**

This law gives consumers the right to know what information is being distributed by a credit bureau. It also gives a consumer rights to correct any erroneous information. The law also requires a creditor who turns down your credit application to tell you which credit bureau provided information that was used in the decision to deny credit.

**Fair Debt Collection Act**

This law prohibits debt collectors from violating your rights by setting forth certain things. Collectors cannot use unfair, abusive, or deceptive practices in collecting overdue bills. The law says what is and is not a reasonable time to call a debtor, prevents deliberate harassment on the job, and so forth.

**Home Equity Consumer Protection Act**

This provides for disclosure of terms of home equity loans and requires a debtor to be informed of the risk of losing his home if the loan is not paid as agreed.

## Appendix B

# Bankruptcy

This information on bankruptcy is in no way intended to explain the laws about bankruptcy. Instead, we will limit our remarks to the practical realities of how bankruptcy affects people, the economy, and the *concept of being responsible.* We will also briefly cover the different kinds of bankruptcy.

There are some people who would lead you to believe that bankruptcy is no big deal and that everybody does it. They say that big-shots and major corporations go bankrupt all the time. They imply that, if you have trouble paying debts, there is no reason you should not file for bankruptcy. These things simply are not true.

In the first place, not many big-shots or corporations go bankrupt. If this were true, our entire economic system would collapse and there would be financial chaos. It is true that a small percent get into trouble and file for protection under bankruptcy laws. Usually this is under *Chapter 11 Reorganization,* which is a special provision in bankruptcy. More on this later.

It is also not true that the majority of everyday people go bankrupt. Again, if this were a fact, there would be economic collapse. There would be no such thing as credit as we know it, nor would there be faith and trust.

There is, however, a bankruptcy law for those who get into financial trouble. That is necessary. There must be some form of legal relief for people who really cannot pay their debts. Many years ago, in England, people were actually put into prison if they did not pay their debts! It was called "debtor's prison." Well, that is not done anymore.

Bankruptcy is not a sugar-coated pill. It is not a cure-all. It is not a "solution" to all financial problems. It should only be considered as a last-chance *alternative* for someone in very serious financial trouble. Even if someone is in desperate trouble and filing bankruptcy becomes necessary, doing so will carry prices and penalties.

## How Bankruptcy Can Affect People

Most importantly, bankruptcy is financial failure. It is not good for people to fail in anything. When they do, there is a tendency to try to justify it. To justify a failure, one must rationalize that he or she couldn't help it or that the failure could not have been avoided. This is a strong human trait, and it is not a healthy one. The very act of rationalizing one failure or mistake makes it easier to justify the next failure or mistake. All of us will encounter adversity in life. Each time we overcome that adversity, we will be the stronger for doing so. We want to build on successes, not justify failures.

We repeat again that bankruptcy is sometimes unavoidable. This is often after the fact, after the mistakes are made and the damage is done. If we get into a serious auto accident and are sued for hundreds of thousands of dollars, maybe the accident could have been avoided. Or, maybe we weren't carrying enough liability insurance. Perhaps we got sick and piled up impossible medical bills. We could have taken better care of our health or had better health insurance.

There are bankruptcies where there is truly no fault of the debtor, but these may be the exception. There was no omission, nor was there anything sensible the person could have done to avoid the problem that caused the impossible amount of debt. Even then, there is still a sense of failure.

The point is that, under most circumstances, bankruptcy is not a good thing. It damages people.

## How Can Someone in Trouble Avoid Bankruptcy?

There are common-sense things that a person tempted to consider bankruptcy should fully explore *first*:

1. Increase income. There are many ways that a well-motivated person can increase income. Lots of people work two jobs and for many reasons. One of the authors has a fine young employee (not in financial trouble) who works two jobs to save money for a down payment on a home.

2. Decrease living expenses. Very few people in true poverty ever get into too much debt. Most credit users have average and often high incomes. People in this class can almost always cut their living expenses a great deal if they are well-motivated to do so.

3. Decrease debt. While this option is seldom a cure-all, many people who get into trouble do so because they buy too many things. There are often possessions that can be disposed of to decrease debt, such as a car, a boat, guns, or whatever. Nothing is as valuable as your pride. Any "goods" given up to help reduce debt can be replaced later in life. Too many people place false pride in possessions.

In addition, anyone having difficulty meeting monthly payments on time should immediately call each creditor and explain the problem. Most creditors are very helpful. But, you must take the first step and communicate.

Finally, we have told you that there are hundreds of non-profit Consumer Credit Counseling Service offices nationwide. If you are sincere and willing to make sacrifices, most can get your creditors to cooperate with a common sense repayment plan that will fit your budget.

## How Does Bankruptcy Affect the Economy?

When someone, or a company, goes bankrupt, the debts don't magically go away. Uncle Sam doesn't pay them. The creditors who are owed must "charge off" the debts. This expression means that money is lost to that business owner or the stockholders. There is a real loss, not a paper one. The only way a business can absorb a loss is to pass it on in the form of higher prices to those who do pay their bills. A business can only raise prices so much and remain competitive. If the business can no longer be competitive, it will lose its customers and go out of business.

There is no free lunch. We are all part of this economic system. If any part of it hurts, we are all hurt. Therefore, bankruptcy is bad for business, and it is bad for you and me.

## The Kinds of Bankruptcy

The federal Bankruptcy Act is a very complicated set of laws. We will give you only a few important highlights. First, we need to tell you something basic about the bankruptcy law. The judge cannot decide if bankruptcy is the right thing for someone to do. The law is simply there. A bankruptcy judge can only rule on what the law says can and cannot be done.

### Chapter 7 Bankruptcy

This is the part of the bankruptcy law under which most petitions are filed. The person, or corporation, seeking relief files a petition with the court. A trustee is appointed by the court to oversee disposition of assets. Once all of the steps and legalities are completed properly, the bankruptcy court grants a discharge. This means that all debts that can legally be discharged by the court no longer must be paid. Not all debts can be discharged. The law provides that a debtor may retain certain necessary assets. Those are referred to as "exempt assets." All assets of the debtor not exempt are turned over to the trustee, who must dispose of them to the benefit of the creditors. The following are some key points about how Chapter 7 affects your debts:

- Student loans and some government backed obligations cannot be discharged by bankruptcy.

- Tax debts are not discharged.

- Responsibility for alimony and child support payments remain.

- Any debts incurred by fraud are not discharged.

- If a debt is co-signed, the co-signer is still fully obligated to repay the debt.

- Secured debts (where a creditor holds collateral) must be dealt with one way or another. If the debtor wishes to keep the collateral, then, with the court's permission, the debt may be reaffirmed. In this event, the debt must be repaid.

### Chapter 13 Bankruptcy

The purpose of a Chapter 13 filing is to provide for repayment of debts under protection of the court. Under this part of bankruptcy law, a debtor may submit a plan for repayment. If approved by the bankruptcy court, creditors can be required to accept the plan. This plan may suit a debtor who has assets he does not wish to lose and has income with which to pay. The bankruptcy court may allow from three to five years to repay the debts.

In areas where there is not a non-profit CCCS that can help, this plan is certainly preferable to a Chapter 7. Chapter 13 is still, however, a bankruptcy filing. It is viewed very negatively by creditors on a credit report. Today, most areas of the country do have a viable CCCS that is supported and cooperated with by creditors. Most creditors, when they find honest customers in trouble, will encourage them to go to a CCCS service.

A major problem with Chapter 13, even with an honest debtor who wants to do the right thing, is that there is no counseling, no education, nor is there treatment of the underlying problem. There is little flexibility. If a person who files a Chapter 13 has trouble meeting the plan, the court may dismiss the plan, and the debtor will be right back into trouble. With a good CCCS program, a full-time professional counselor is assigned to the case. Problems can be worked out, and creditors are usually happy to cooperate. A CCCS plan is *voluntary* and does not involve the courts or lawyers.

### Chapter 11

This plan is not for typical consumers, although it can apply to a few. The purpose of Chapter 11 is to give a company (or the individual) in financial trouble a chance to reorganize their finances. Their goal is to become profitable again and save their company. Some Chapter 11s are successful, and the company later thrives. Others are not successful and fall into Chapter 7.

When you hear of a company filing for bankruptcy, it is often filing a Chapter 11 reorganization. In a Chapter 11 reorganization, a company is afforded an immediate reprieve from creditors. It must, within a certain time period, file a plan to reorganize with the bankruptcy court. This plan must be very comprehensive. It must spell out exactly how the company proposes to deal with its debts and obligations and how it proposes to operate while under the protection of the court. A trustee may be appointed, and often the court has much to say about what the company can and cannot do in running its business during the reorganization. The creditors have certain rights in the proceedings. If a plan is approved, then the company may operate within that plan in their efforts to become a solvent company again.

### Chapter 12 and Other Chapters

Chapter 12 is a special part of the bankruptcy law designed exclusively for farmers. There are other chapters for railroads and a few other special cases.

### Food for Thought

Creditors agree that there must be some form of a bankruptcy law. Creditors agree that even prudent and responsible people can (but rarely) find themselves saddled with an impossible amount of debt. A serious health problem, disability, or accident can wipe a person out financially. Then, too, an extended period of unemployment on top of heavy debt can bring hardship—even for someone who may have had savings.

Many feel that the present bankruptcy laws do not constructively address the need. These laws originated many years ago when nearly all credit was heavily secured with collateral. Times have changed. Credit today is primarily extended on faith, trust, and the promise to repay out of future income—even when there is collateral. While many bankruptcies today cannot be avoided, there is growing concern that too many people use bankruptcy as an easy way out of debts that they made to purchase goods and services.

## According to Webster

**Bankrupt (noun):** 1a: a person who has done any of the acts that by law entitle his creditors to have his estate administered for their benefit b: a person judicially declared subject to having his estate administered under the bankrupt laws for the benefit of his creditors c: a person who becomes insolvent 2: one who is destitute of a particular thing (a moral).

**Bankrupt (adj):** 1a: reduced to a state of financial ruin: IMPOVERISHED: legally declared a bankrupt b: of or relating to bankrupts or bankruptcy 2a: BROKEN, RUINED (a...professional career) b: exhausted of valuable qualities: STERILE c: destitute.

**Bankruptcy (noun):** 1: the quality or state of being bankrupt 2: utter failure or impoverishment.

Source: *Webster's Ninth New Collegiate Dictionary*

# Appendix C

# Consumer Credit Counseling Services

There was a time when, if a person got too deep into debt, there was no place to turn except to the lawyers and the bankruptcy court. That time was before the concept of non-profit Consumer Credit Counseling Services came to life over 30 years ago. Today, there is face-to-face, non-profit help available to nearly everyone in the country.

There are more than 200 autonomous CCCS services that operate over 1,200 offices across the country. Autonomous means that each is a separate corporation with its own board of directors. All share a common mission: money management and credit counseling, Debt Management Programs for those with serious financial problems, and educational programs teaching and promoting the responsible use of credit.

These CCCS offices are able to play a beneficial role because:

- Most people who experience financial difficulty are honest and want to repay their debts. Thank goodness!

- The creditors they owe are responsible business people. They much prefer to see their customers get help, and will both cooperate with and financially support the non-profit CCCS services.

- CCCS services are independent, neutral third-parties, and thus are able to work with all concerned to reach common goals.

- Even though most people seen by CCCS are financially over-obligated, they have incomes and are not destitute. Although they may be in trouble, there is usually income to work with. By tailoring and administering a realistic, disciplined budget and obtaining the cooperation of creditors, the debts gradually can be repaid.

## How Are CCCS Services Governed?

All CCCS services are governed by local boards of directors made up from all segments of the community. These directors are leading citizens and business people active in community affairs. These men and women serve without compensation. Their role is to set policy, direction, and goals. A board employs a president or executive director who is charged with carrying out the mission of the service. This chief executive is responsible for managing the affairs of the program and staffing the agency with counselors and the many other employees who are necessary for the agency to deliver its services.

Every CCCS in the country is a member of the National Foundation for Consumer Credit. This umbrella organization helps local CCCS programs in many ways. The NFCC helps coordinate creditor cooperation and financial support for the individual services, fosters educational programs, helps new services get started, and provides other support services for members.

## How Are CCCS Services Funded?

Non-profit agencies must have income with which to operate, just as any other business must have. That income must exceed expenses so that they may have operating capital. The majority of income of CCCS services comes from responsible creditors who know that some honest customers may one day encounter financial difficulties. Quite naturally, businesses want these customers to be able to get help so they can pay their bills. Perhaps even more important, most businesses truly want to help for humanitarian reasons. It's good for the community, for the economy, for all concerned. We have already told you that the alternative, bankruptcy, is bad for everyone.

Most services have small user fees in one form or another. There may be a small fee for initial counseling. If the problems are serious and a debt management program is needed, there may be a small cost to help defray administering a plan. We cover this later.

Some services are a part of United Way and get part of their income from that source. There can be other, sometimes important sources of income, depending upon the community in which the service is established. But, the majority of income is contributed by business creditors.

## What Services Can a CCCS Provide?

The most important services are counseling, educational programs, and where necessary, a long-term debt management program for someone in serious trouble.

Many people in financial trouble can be helped by counseling alone. There are problems, but with advice, the client can solve his or her problem. In serious cases, there may be obstacles that the client may not be able to overcome alone. In the case of severe over-obligation, the client may need the service to contact creditors and arrange payments within his or her means. In such a case, an arrangement may be made with a client for a sensible living expense budget, with the remainder of income being administered by the agency with the cooperation of creditors.

CCCS agencies provide many educational services. These services include not only counseling to individual clients, but programs for the general public. These programs take a variety of forms, usually including seminars, distribution of information on budgeting and the wise use of credit, and sometimes classes taught in schools. Seminars offered may cover a variety of topics. They may range from classes on budgeting to first-time home buying programs.

## How Can Someone in Need Get Help From a CCCS?

In most cases, help is but a phone call away. Nearly every CCCS service in the country is easily accessible and strives to give appointments for counseling very quickly. Procedures may vary slightly, but the first thing for someone to do is pick up the phone and call the nearest service. In larger communities, look in the white pages under Consumer Credit Counseling Service. If this doesn't do the trick, call the Better Business Bureau if one is in your area, or call one of the larger creditors you may owe. When you make contact with the CCCS program in your area, a representative will answer your questions about getting an appointment. You may be requested to fill out a simple information form to have ready for your appointment.

When a CCCS counselor meets with a client, the goal is to understand the problems and find sensible ways to deal with them. It may take one or more meetings with a counselor to do this. As we mentioned earlier, many people can be assisted simply by counseling. In other, more serious cases, a debt management plan may be recommended. In all cases, working with a CCCS program is voluntary.

A realistic note here. In serious cases, there is no easy solution. Excessive debt, often accumulated over a period of years, will not magically go away. Sincere people, who wish to meet the situation they created, may have to make sensible sacrifices to live within a budget in order to repay debts. But only through meeting adversity head on and overcoming it can any of us build our strengths. No one gets through this life without bumps and bruises, and all too often they involve money. Every time we meet challenge and succeed, we are the stronger and better for it. If, on the other hand, we make excuses to justify a failure, we become prone to making the same mistakes again and again.

# CONSUMER CREDIT COUNSELING

# SERVICE POLICIES

**Consumer Credit Counseling Service Members Shall:**

- operate as a non-profit community service.

- provide confidential and professional budget and debt management counseling in a non-discriminatory manner.

- develop and foster community educational programs on money management, budgeting, and the intelligent use of credit.

- make services available and affordable, ensuring no one be denied access to programs because of inability to pay.

- provide a debt management program, when appropriate, which is most beneficial to the client and fair to all creditors.

- maintain fiscal responsibility to ensure integrity and community trust.

- maintain broad-based community representation on its governing board.

# Appendix D

## Better Business Bureaus

BBBs, like Consumer Credit Counseling Services, are non-profit community service organizations. Their boards function much the same as in the case of CCCS programs, serving without compensation.

A BBB is sponsored by private business and is dedicated to the public interest serving business, consumers, and the marketplace.

### What Services does a BBB Provide?

A BBB provides a variety of services to the public and also to businesses. Among them are the following.

### *Inquiries*

A consumer, or a business, wishing to check the background of someone he or she is considering doing business with, may telephone the local BBB for a report. This report will provide background information on a business as well as its track record regarding customer complaints. This information can really help a consumer avoid a possibly unhappy experience if he or she will call the BBB *before* doing business with an unknown firm.

The BBB will also provide reports on organizations which solicit donations.

If you call inquiring about a company who is not on file with the BBB, the BBB will try to develop a report or refer you to another BBB which may have information.

## Complaints

The BBB has experienced personnel who can assist with advice or consumer-related complaints. A BBB will require that you put a complaint in writing. Only in that way can they act on it. When a complaint is filed, the BBB will immediately contact the business involved. Every effort will be made to resolve the dispute. This process may take only a few days or up to several weeks. Even the most responsible business is, sooner or later, going to displease a customer. When this occurs, the business usually is very cooperative with a BBB in resolving things to everyone's satisfaction.

## Arbitration

The Better Business Bureau administers an arbitration program. This procedure is often successful in resolving a dispute that could not be handled by normal procedures.

In these cases, trained volunteer arbitrators conduct a hearing and render a decision which is binding on each party who has agreed to the arbitration. Many national companies have standing agreements with BBBs to be willing to arbitrate any dispute.

Arbitration is an excellent program. It offers a means to resolve problems without involving lawyers and courts.

## Advertising Review

The BBB has an ongoing program of monitoring advertising. This is a means of helping to maintain accuracy and honesty in advertising. Whenever an ad appears to be deceptive or misleading or not in compliance with advertising codes, the BBB will contact the advertiser. The purpose is to assist an honest merchant to make any appropriate changes. This is a voluntary, self-regulation program.

## Membership

A BBB is financially supported by business firms which meet and maintain certain standards. All firms are pre-screened before being invited to be a member of the BBB. All applications for membership in the BBB must be approved by the BBB's board of directors.

The more a BBB is used by the public, the better its services are! Any consumer feeling he or she has a valid complaint with a business firm *should* call the BBB. The BBB may be able to solve the problem for the consumer. If it is a legitimate complaint and the merchant will not attempt to correct the problem, the complaint is filed and reported to the next consumer inquiring about that business. In this way, the BBB builds a favorable file on businesses who serve the public fairly, and builds a complaint file on those who are not responsive.

# Appendix E

# Gambling—Recreation or Addiction?

Gambling is mentioned in this book for two reasons. First, gambling is so much more accessible to so many more people. Second, gambling can have a devastating impact on one's financial life.

A few short years ago, if you wanted to gamble, you had to go to Las Vegas or to one of the very few other places in America where gambling was legal. That has changed.

Our purpose here is not moralistic. We are not going to try to convince you that gambling is evil or wrong. Gambling has been around as long as dirt. Like a lot of other things in life, if taken in moderation, gambling may not hurt you. Our purpose is to simply to arm you with information.

Experience has proven that some people cannot deal with any form of gambling, even in small doses. For those people, it quickly becomes an addictive compulsion. When that happens, it quickly dominates and destroys their lives. Also, gambling often destroys the lives of people around them as well.

The same thing happens with alcohol. Most people can take an occasional drink and leave it alone the rest of the time.

Others must practice complete abstinence or alcohol will over-whelm them.

Gambling will hurt you financially because the deck is stacked against you! In any form of commercial gambling, you are not supposed to win. The game, and the odds, are carefully controlled so that you will lose. Otherwise, the people who own the gambling enterprises would lose. Out of every dollar that is gambled, a certain amount must go to pay for overhead (the expenses of the facility, salaries, and so on), a certain amount for taxes, and another amount for profit to the owners. That does not leave much to be returned to the players in the form of winnings!

Gambling is a multi-billion-dollar industry. Owners of casinos, river boats, video poker machines, and other gam-bling facilities are not taking chances. They are in control of the odds—you are not. They are after profits—and these profits must come from the players.

Again, we are not preaching morality—just reality. The chances of you winning big bucks are close to zero. Even the highly-publicized state lotteries are, in the words of a well-known, self-admitted gambler, "a sucker's bet."

We could fill this book with facts on gambling—odds, numbers, you name it. To give you a small glimpse of what is going on, we will state but one example. Louisiana is not a large nor a rich state. With just a little more than four million people, the "take" on video poker machines in Louisiana in 1994 was nearly $500 million! The "take" is not the amount of money placed in these machines, *but the amount lost!* If that's how you want to spend your money—it's a free country.

If you are of legal age and your budget can afford a few recreational dollars, then that's another matter. Spend those recreation dollars however you choose. Just understand that, if you try to gamble with anything other than recreation in mind, you will lose more than your budget can stand.

## Appendix F

# Your Vote, Your Voice — Make it Heard

This book is about you and how you can make yourself better financially. We cover things that affect your pocketbook. You've read about taxes — how the government takes your money and spends that money. So, you will want to have a voice in government. You will want to affect how government taxes and spends. In other words, you will want to vote.

If you are not yet 18, you will be before you know it. At one time in America, you had to be 21 before you got the right to vote. You could go to war to defend your freedom before you could vote. Back then, a great majority of kids looked forward to when they could vote. It represented an achievement, or rite of passage, so to speak. We wonder if that's true any more. Voting records tell us that there has been a disturbing trend in the past generation, with fewer and fewer people exercising their right to vote.

If that dangerous trend continues, fewer and fewer people will be deciding the future of this great country. As politicians learn that people no longer take an active role in what laws are passed, they will take greater liberties in deciding what they think is best for you. That is dangerous. They will be more and more accountable to the fewer people that do vote—and less accountable to the people who don't vote. That is dangerous.

That trend must be reversed if this country is to continue in its tradition as the greatest country in the world. What do you think has made us the greatest country in the world? Our people, our form of government, and our right to vote.

The voting trend can be reversed—but only starting with you. So, if or when you are 18, vote. If you don't know who to vote for, or even what you would be voting about, ask other people. Ask your relatives, your friends, your employer—anyone you look up to. Read, read, and read. Take a position. Find out what each politician, or each candidate for office, stands for. Then, take your position and vote. Your vote does not have to be a correct one by anyone else's opinion. That is the beauty of our system.

If you do not vote, you have lost your voice.

By the way, if you don't think this is such a great country, then can you tell us why most of the rest of the world would love to come here?

# Appendix G

# Glossary

**ATM** — An automated teller machine which accepts deposits and allows withdrawals from accounts at depository institutions.

**Annual Percentage Rate** — The interest rate on loans calculated uniformly as provided in the Truth in Lending Act so that borrowers can compare interest rates charged by different lenders.

**Assets** — What a person owns.

**Assigned Risk** — Individuals who have a bad driving record in terms of tickets and accidents and who cannot get regular insurance are put into an assigned risk pool, and insurance is provided at high premiums.

**Availability of Funds** — The delay which a depository institution may impose on your access to funds after you have deposited checks drawn against another depository institution.

**Balance Sheet** — A snapshot of a person's financial condition as of a certain date. It shows a person's assets, liabilities, and net worth.

**Balancing the Checkbook** — The process of proving that the individual depositor's records agree with the bank statement.

**Borrower** — One who gives a promise to repay in a credit transaction. (See Debtor)

**Borrowing Money** — A way to get money by exchanging a promise to repay in the future.

**Capacity** — In terms of credit, a person's ability to borrow and repay money as determined by his or her disposable income.

**Capital** — Tools, equipment, factories, and the like which workers need to produce goods and services. Capital is one of the factors of production.

**Capital Gains** — An increase in the market value of a corporation stock which a person owns. As the market price of a stock goes up, the owner can have capital gains if he or she sells the stock at a price higher than he or she paid for it.

**Car Insurance** — Insurance policies which insure some of the risks involved in owning and operating an automobile.

**Character** — A person's reputation for being reliable, ethical, and dependable.

**Checking Account** — An account at a depository institution which can be used as a convenient payments mechanism.

**Choices** — Because not everyone can have everything that he or she wants nor do everything that he or she would like, each of us must make choices. We must choose the things or activities that we can attain from a large number of possible things or activities.

**Collateral** — Something of value, such as a car, a home, or savings, pledged as security on a loan.

**Collision and Comprehensive** — A type of automobile insurance that pays for damage to your car by vandalism, fire, or theft.

**Collision Insurance** — An insurance policy that pays to fix your car if you have a wreck whether or not it is your fault.

**Co-maker** — A co-signer. (See Co-signing)

**Commercial Bank**—A type of depository institution which offers to the public a broad array of services, including loans and deposits and other financial services.

**Consumer Credit Counseling Service**—A non-profit community service organization which helps people deal with credit problems. The service is available in all major cities in Louisiana and throughout the United States.

**Consumer Finance Company**—A type of entrepreneurial financial institution which specializes in small loans to individuals who may not be able to get credit at depository institutions.

**Contractual Financial Institutions**—People make payments to these institutions over a period of time and can get their money out only when a particular event, such as retirement or death, occurs.

**Co-signing**—The act of promising to repay another person's debt if that person will not or cannot repay.

**Credit**—Granting of money or something else of value in exchange for a promise to repay at some time in the future.

**Credit Application**—A form on which a potential borrower provides important information to a potential lender.

**Credit Bureau**—A company that gathers information on people who use credit and sells that information to companies that grant credit.

**Credit Capacity**—The total amount of credit which an individual or business firm can expect to have based primarily on the borrower's character, capacity, and capital.

**Credit Cards**—Plastic cards through which a financial institution substitutes its credit for that of the card holder, which enables the card holder to buy goods and services on credit.

**Credit Life Insurance**—An insurance policy which repays loans should the borrower die or become disabled.

**Credit Report** — The information which credit bureaus sell to companies that grant credit.

**Credit Union** — A depository financial institution which is owned by the members. Credit unions offer a wide array of loans and deposit products and other financial services.

**Creditor** — One who extends credit.

**Debit Card** — A card used like a credit card to make a purchase, except that the purchase price is immediately deducted from the user's checking account balance; like an electronic check.

**Debtor** — One who gives a promise to repay. (See Borrower)

**Deductible** — In insurance, a specified amount of damages or claim which must be exceeded before the insurance company pays. The insurance company pays the amount above the deductible.

**Dependent** — In tax terminology, someone who qualifies to be claimed on your tax return for an "Exemption," allowing a specified amount to be subtracted from taxable income. There are many rules governing who may be claimed as a dependant.

**Depository Financial Institutions** — Institutions in which a person deposits money and can withdraw it upon demand.

**Disposable Income** — Income which is neither needed to meet living expenses nor already committed for other debt.

**Disclosure Statement** — A form which shows the borrower all costs of the transaction, including interest rate.

**Dividends** — Profit distributions by corporations to shareholders who own stock in the corporations.

**Down Payment** — Some of the borrower's own money which, along with money borrowed from a lender, is used to buy a good, such as a house or a car.

**Earned Income Credit** — A special provision in federal income tax law that can actually pay money, to qualifying persons, even though no taxes were paid or due.

**Earning Money** — One of the ways a person gets money is earning it through providing labor in a job.

**Endorsements** — The process of signing the back of a check to make another individual the payee.

**Endorser** — One who co-signs a note or extends his or her credit to repay the loan of another if that borrower cannot or will not repay. (See Co-signing)

**Entrepreneurial Financial Institutions** — Companies which borrow money elsewhere and lend it to individuals.

**Entrepreneurship** — The creative act of putting together the five factors of production to produce goods and services.

**Equity** — The difference between what a person owns as of a given date and what that person owes. (See Net Worth.)

**Exemption** — In tax terminology, a deduction (of an amount) from taxable income for yourself and each eligible dependent.

**Factors of Production** — Five types of things (land, labor, capital, resources, and technology) which are required to produce every good and service.

**Fair Credit Reporting Act** — A federal law giving individuals the right to find out what is contained in their credit report at credit bureaus, and a procedure to correct any erroneous information.

**Form 1040EZ** — A federal tax form. The shortest, simplest form of all. Can be used only by a single taxpayer with no dependents.

**Form 1040A** — A federal tax form. For use by a taxpayer who has an income under $50,000 and does not itemize deductions.

**Form 1040** — A federal tax form for use by anyone who cannot file a 1040EZ or 1040A. The most complicated form.

**Form 1099** — A federal tax form, somewhat similar to a W-2 in purpose. It is used to report income from sources other than wages. An example is interest; a savings institution must send you a 1099 at the end of the year disclosing interest paid to you.

**Functions of Money** — Money serves as a medium of exchange that can be used to buy goods and services. Money also serves as a store of value in that it allows people to buy things at some time in the future. It also serves as a measure of value.

**Goals** — Desirable and worthwhile objectives which we seek to attain or accomplish.

**Having Good Credit** — The ability of a person to borrow readily.

**Head of Household** — A special tax filing status, qualifying eligible single persons for a lower tax rate.

**Health Insurance** — A type of insurance that pays, according to the terms of the policy, for medical and/or hospitalization costs.

**Health and Accident Insurance** — Not to be confused with true, broad coverage Health Insurance. This coverage is usually very limited and pays specific limited amounts for events specified in the policy.

**Income Tax** — A type of tax on the income of individuals. In the U.S., often the largest amount of tax paid by individuals, except for those who have low incomes. Imposed by the federal government and many states.

**Income Tax Rate** — A percentage applied against taxable income to determine taxes owed. The rate varies according to income levels.

**Inflation** — When there is too much money in the economy and this money is used by people to attempt to buy a limited supply of goods and services. That condition results in higher prices. Increasing prices is called inflation.

**Installment Loan** — A loan which the borrower pays back in periodic, usually monthly, payments.

**Insurance Discounts** — The discounted (reduced) premium on automobile insurance for a variety of reasons, such as being a good driver, being a good student, having taken drivers education, and the like.

**Interest** — The price of credit. Interest is compensation to lenders paid by borrowers.

**Interest Rates** — The amount of interest expressed as a percentage of the amount of money being borrowed.

**Internal Revenue Service** — The branch of the federal government charged with the responsibility for collecting income tax. Abbreviated "IRS."

**Insurance** — The process of transferring risk to others by buying a policy.

**Labor** — People's work or effort in the productive process. Labor is one of the factors of production.

**Land** — The geographical space which is required for the production of every good or service. Land is one of the factors of production.

**Law of Demand** — The economic principle that people buy more as the price of a good or service goes down. As the price of a good or service goes up, people buy less.

**Liability Insurance** — Insurance that pays for injuries or damage you may cause.

**Liabilities** — What a person owes.

**Life Insurance**—Policies which pay upon the death of the insured or, in some instances, the occasion of other events.

**Life Insurance Company**—A type of contractual financial institution to which a policy holder makes payments and gets his or her money out upon the occurrence of some event such as death.

**Limits of Liability**—An insurance term. The maximum amount(s) the insurance company is obligated to pay for damages you cause.

**Luxuries of Life**—Goods and services such as a diamond ring or membership in a health club which are nice to have but are not required for existence.

**Market**—The way people behave in an economic way. The term also means a place where buying and selling take place.

**Measure of Value**—A function of money by which we gauge the relative differences between things such as incomes, prices, and wealth.

**Medical Payments Coverage**—This part of an insurance policy covers you and anyone in your car for medical payments up to set limits.

**Medium of Exchange**—A function of money by which people use money to buy goods and services.

**Money**—Anything which is generally accepted as a medium of exchange or a store of value is money.

**Money—How You Get It**—Money can be earned, borrowed, or received as a gift.

**Money Market Mutual Funds**—A relatively new depository financial institution which invests a saver's funds in short-term market securities.

**Maturity**—The length of a loan.

**NSF Check**—When a person writing a check does not have sufficient funds in his or her checking account to cover the amount of the check.

**Necessities of Life**—Goods and services such as food, shelter, clothes, and medical care which are required for existence.

**Net Worth**—The difference between what a person owns as of a given date and what that person owes. (See Equity)

**Outstanding Check**—A check which has been written but has not yet been paid against the account by the depository institution.

**Overdraft**—A negative balance in a checking account caused by a person who writes a check for which there is not enough money in the account.

**Pension Funds**—A contractual financial institution to which savers make periodic deposits and get the money out upon the occasion of retirement, death, or some other event.

**Price**—The value of any good or service (including labor) which is determined in the marketplace.

**Production**—The process of combining factors of production to produce goods and services.

**Property Insurance**—Often referred to as a "Homeowner's Policy." This insurance affords protection against fire, theft, storm damages, and the like. Includes liability insurance for the homeowner as well.

**Reconciling Item**—An item, usually something like a service charge or charge for printed checks, which must be taken into account when balancing the checkbook.

**Residential Insurance**—Insurance which offers protection to people who own their own homes or rent apartments or homes.

**Resources** — Natural things such as wood, oil, iron, or hydrogen which are required in the production of every good or service. Resources represent a factor of production.

**Return on Savings** — A way of earning money by investing money in order to receive interest.

**Savings and Loan Associations** — Depository financial institutions which primarily provide credit for purchasing homes. They offer other financial products as well.

**Scarcity** — Factors of production are limited, and only a limited volume of goods and services can be produced in any society. There is scarcity because everything is not available in unlimited supplies.

**Social Security Tax** — A federal tax on earnings, deducted from wages by an employer and paid to the government. For 1995, the rate paid by workers is 7.65 percent on the first $61,200 of earnings. This same tax amount must be matched and paid by employers.

**Standard Deduction** — A tax term. All taxpayers are entitled to this deduction. The amount varies according to filing status and can vary by tax year.

**Store of Value** — A function of money which allows people to buy things in the future.

**Tax Credit** — Not to be confused with a tax deduction. A credit is an amount that can be subtracted directly from taxes due.

**Tax Liability** — In federal income taxes, the total amount of tax owed for the year, whether this amount was withheld from earnings or not.

**Tax Return** — A form, either federal or state, containing information that must be reported to the government. Used to compute any tax owed, and covers a specific tax period — usually a calendar year.

**Tax Withholding**—An amount, determined by the W-4 form completed by an employee, that is held out of a paycheck. If the W-4 is accurately completed, the employer will hold out an amount of tax that will closely match the employee's tax liability for the year.

**Taxable Income**—The amount of income upon which tax must be paid. The amount after all allowances for deductions and exemptions.

**Technology**—Knowledge or know-how required to produce every good or service. Technology is one of the factors of production.

**Term Insurance**—The simplest and cheapest of life insurance policies which provides protection against death only and does not build up cash value.

**Term Loan**—A loan which the borrower pays back in full all at once at the end of an agreed time.

**Transit Item**—A deposit which a person has made but which has not yet been posted to his or her bank account.

**Uninsured Motorists Insurance**—A part of an automobile policy which covers injuries to you and your passengers caused by another driver who does not have insurance.

**W-2**—A form that an employer must send to each employee reporting earnings and tax information for the prior year. This form is necessary for completing a tax return.

**W-4**—A form that an employee must complete and furnish his or her employer. The information tells the employer how much federal income tax to withhold each payday. An employee can fill out a new W-4 for the employer to use anytime the employee's tax circumstances change.

**Wages**—The price of labor.

**Whole Life Insurance**—A type of life insurance which provides death benefits and which builds up "cash value" over the life of the policy.

# Index